A THREAD OF

Copyright © 2024 by Suprise Žihlavski.

All rights reserved. No part of this book may be used or reproduced in any form whatsoever without written permission except in the case of brief quotations in critical articles or reviews.

All Scripture quotations, unless otherwise indicated, are taken from the Holy Bible, New International Version®, NIV®. Copyright ©1973, 1978, 1984, 2011 by Biblica, Inc. ™ Used by permission of Zondervan. All rights reserved worldwide.

For more information, or to book an event, email : zihlavskisurprise@gmail.com

Cover design by Vladimir Žihlavski

ISBN - Paperback: 978-0-7961-7273-0

CONTENTS

Introduction   9

1. Did God really say?   15

2. The faith of Sarah   27

3. The faith of Rebekah   37

4. The faith of Leah   46

5. The faith of the Midwives   54

6. The faith of Jochebed   63

7. The faith of Zipporah   70

8. The faith of Rahab   78

9. The faith of Deborah   84

10. The faith of Manoah's wife   91

11. The faith of Ruth   97

12. The faith of Hannah   106

13. The faith Abigail   112

14. The faith of Queen Jezebel   121

15. The faith of the Widow   128

16. The faith of the Captive Maid   135

17. The faith of Queen Athaliah   144

18. The faith of Jehosheba   151

19. The faith of Queen Esther   157

20. The faith of Elisabeth   166

21. The faith of Mary   174

22. The faith of Anna   184

23. The faith of the Bleeding Woman   190

24. The faith of the Cannanite Woman   198

25. The faith of the Samaritan Woman   206

26. The faith of Mary of Bethany   213

27. The faith of Mary Magdalene   220

EPILOGUE   230

PRAYER   233

ABOUT AUTHOR   235

ACKNOWLEDGMENTS   236

FAITH SCRIPTURES   237

INTRODUCTION

This book tells the inspiring stories of regular women who played crucial roles in fulfilling God's plan of redemption. Through their faith and obedience to God, these women became vital instruments in His purpose, leading to significant events that ultimately resulted in the manifestation of this plan of redemption fulfilled in Jesus Christ, the Redeemer.

Each chapter delves into these women's unique circumstances, challenges, and victories, emphasizing their faith in God and pivotal roles in His plan. The book's narrative commences by recounting the story of Eve, the first woman who walked with God and trusted in Him. However, Eve's faith in God wavered, leading to humanity's separation from Him.

As the book progresses, God's plan for redemption unfolds gradually, and the book highlights the stories of several women whose faith paved the way for the fulfillment of this plan. These women's stories inspire us to trust God and His son, Jesus Christ. By doing so, our faith becomes like a thread that God can use to weave His plans and purposes into the world. This book is a heartwarming reminder that God's plan includes ordinary people who become instruments of His purpose.

In a world that frequently values fame, power, and recognition, this book reminds us that we can find true significance in a relationship with God, faith in Him, and obedience to Him. By having faith, God empowers us to fulfill His plans and purposes for the salvation of humanity.

INTRODUCTION

Defining Terms

What is Redemption?

Redemption refers to saving or being saved from sin, evil, and the consequences of sin, which is separation from God in Hell (see Luke 16:22–23). In the Christian context, redemption is the process by which God delivers humanity and all of creation from the power of sin and death through the sacrifice of Jesus Christ on the cross and His resurrection from the dead (see Titus 2:14 and 1 Peter 1:14-18). This sacrifice is the ultimate expression of God's love and mercy towards humanity, demonstrating the extent to which God was willing to restore humanity to a right relationship with Him.

Redemption begins with faith in Jesus Christ's death on the cross for the forgiveness of sins and repentance, where individuals acknowledge their sinful nature and turn away from their past sins (see 1 Corinthians 6:9-11). Through this process, they receive forgiveness for their sins and are restored to a right relationship with God.

The Rewards of Redemption

To be redeemed is to undergo a profound spiritual transformation that results in a rebirth of the soul. This process is characterized by several critical elements that work together to bring about a profound change in the individual. At the heart of redemption is forgiveness, which allows us to release our burdens of guilt and shame (see Ephesians 1:7).

In addition to forgiveness, redemption also involves justification, which is the process by which we are declared righteous by God in Christ (see Galatians 2:16 and Romans 5:1). To be declared righteous by God involves recognizing our sinfulness and a willingness to turn away from our old ways and embrace a new life in Christ. Through this process of justification, we are set free from the bondage of sin and given the gift of eternal life.

Redemption is also characterized by adoption, the

process by which God welcomes believers into His family. Through adoption, we become heirs to all God's promises and blessings and are given a new identity as children of God (see Ephesians 1:4-5).

Also, redemption involves reconciliation, the process by which we are brought back from being God's enemies through faith in Jesus into a right relationship with God. Through reconciliation, we experience the fullness of God's love and grace, and we can live our lives with Him in a way that is pleasing to Him (see Romans 5:10).

Finally, redemption leads to eternal life, which knows no end. Through eternal life, we escape the grasp of death. Though our bodies may perish, we continue to live on. This life does not begin when we die. It is now, as scripture states, "whoever believes in the Son has eternal life" (John 3:36).

On the other hand, those who don't have Jesus Christ may have their bodies alive, but they are spiritually dead. Even after their physical death, they will experience eternal separation from God, known as the second death, as stated in Revelation

21:8. Ultimately, redemption is a transformative process that changes us from within, giving us a new life and an eternal relationship with God.

1

DID GOD REALLY SAY?

The Garden of Eden was an extraordinary and beautiful place filled with abundant life. It was an oasis of colorful flowers and greenery, with the sweet sound of birds singing in the air. The tall trees stood firm, and their evergreen branches stretched towards the bright blue sky like they were reaching to the heavens. The trees had ripe fruits ready for the taking, and the garden was full of vegetables and plants that grew in abundance. Animals roamed freely, filling the air with their sounds. As Eve walked along the paths, she must have felt a sense of peace and happiness. She lacked nothing and knew it was all because of God's goodness. God's presence surrounded her, giving her a sense of safety and security that only He could provide.

I imagine her loving husband, Adam, by her side, and together, they walked, talked, and laughed, enjoying the garden's beauty and God's ever-present presence. As they strolled hand in hand, they gazed up at the sky, filled with awe and gratitude for who God is and all the blessings He has given them.

Eve's Faith

Eve was delighted and content because she believed in God. This faith gave her a strong foundation and the courage to overcome adversity. With her faith as her anchor, she navigated life's challenges quickly and gracefully. I envision Eve spending her days expressing gratitude to God and filling the garden with her voice through songs of praise and worship. Adam joined in, and together, they sang a beautiful melody, their voices echoing with God's creation that existed to show and exalt His goodness.

Eve is Deceived

One day, a cunning serpent scanned its surroundings, searching for an opportunity to approach Eve. As Eve wandered through the garden, the snake slithered up to her and insidiously implanted a seed of mistrust in her mind. "Did God really say that you must not eat from any tree in the garden?" the serpent cunningly questioned (Genesis 3:1). While Eve knew the truth — the serpent's words activated a yearning within her, even though God had forbidden her from consuming the fruit of the tree in the garden. Until now, Eve had always obeyed God's command, but after listening to the serpent's lies, she began to see the tree in a different light and entertain the idea of disobeying God.

Eve's Disobedience

It wasn't long before the serpent convinced Eve that

she and her husband needed more than they already had and that God was withholding good from them. As a result, her faith, confidence, and loyalty to God began to waver, and she slowly reached out for the forbidden fruit. After eating the fruit, Adam and Eve realized they were naked, and everything changed. They knew what they had done was wrong and felt deep regret and fear. As they heard God walking in the garden, they hastily hid, knowing they could no longer bear to face Him in their state of sin. The once blissful garden became a place of shame and guilt, as their disobedience had led to the loss of their innocence and the introduction of sin and death into the world. Adam and Eve doubted God's goodness and, therefore, sought to attain what they thought was suitable for them by disobeying God.

God's Plan for Redemption

The consequences of Eve's sin of mistrust and disobedience were far-reaching and continue to affect humanity today. However, despite the dire circumstances, Christianity shows that God has a plan for redemption. This plan for redemption involves the sacrifice of Jesus Christ, who died on the cross to pay the penalty for the sins of humanity. Through His death and resurrection, humanity can be forgiven and redeemed. The death and the resurrection of Jesus are the central message of Christianity and provide hope and assurance for those who believe in it.

Throughout the upcoming chapters, you will have the opportunity to read the stories of women who, through their faith, played a crucial role in God's plan for human redemption. Additionally, you will come across several stories of women who had the privilege of experiencing the redeeming power of Jesus Christ firsthand. These accounts serve as a testament to the transformative nature of faith and its profound impact on our lives.

Encouragement

> "Oh, taste and see that the Lord is good; Blessed is the man who trusts in Him! Oh, fear

the Lord, you His saints! There is no want to those who fear Him." Psalm 34:8-9 (NKJV)

Many women today continue to fall into the same trap, and the underlying cause of all sin remains unchanged: lack of faith and contentment. In Genesis 3:5, the serpent tempted Eve by suggesting that if she were to eat from the forbidden tree, she would become like God and possess knowledge of good and evil. How often do we, like Eve, desire forbidden knowledge? We frequently find ourselves contemplating what the future holds for us, whether our suffering will persist indefinitely or if we will find success in our endeavors.

These questions plague our minds, causing sleepless nights. But why, dear sister, do we strive to uncover what God has chosen to keep hidden? Why do we yearn to comprehend what God has decided not to reveal? You may argue that you have the right to know why your child passed away, why your marriage ended, or why you must endure so much suffering. However, the crucial question is whether we genuinely believe in God and His goodness. If we truly believe in God's goodness, even in times of suffering and despair, we would not seek knowledge beyond what He has already revealed or desire things that He has not given. Instead, we would find comfort in His kindness, knowing we are aligned with His perfect will.

A heart that harbors doubt towards God paves the way for sin.

Our purpose is not to doubt but rather to trust in God and find comfort in knowing He is good and everything He does is good. Even though we may not always comprehend or see His plans, we can be sure they are for our benefit because of His inherent goodness. However, when doubt creeps into our hearts, it has the potential to open the door to sin in our lives. We resort to lying because we lack faith in

God's ability to support us if we speak the truth. We steal and covet because we are dissatisfied with the blessings God has already bestowed upon us. We engage in immoral acts because we doubt God's intentions and timing for our lives.

In moments of despair, we may even contemplate suicide because we question God's faithfulness in guiding us through pain, sorrow, and discouragement. Furthermore, we may question our own identity, believing that God made a mistake in creating us as a certain gender. These sinful actions stem from the deceptive vision that the devil, just as he did with Eve, has sold us – a vision that suggests there is something better out there, that God is not truly good, and that He withholds goodness from us.

> *"Faith does not eliminate questions. But faith knows where to take them."* -Elisabeth Elliot

As Christian women, we often find it hard to maintain steadfast faith in God. Sometimes, our trust weakens, and we might experience doubts and uncertainties. At such moments of weakness, it is easy to give in to doubts and fears instead of trusting in God. However, it is important to remember that, taking the easy way out is not beneficial for us. Instead, we should choose to do what is difficult and continue to believe that God is good and that, everything He allows or withholds from us is for our good — even when everything around us seems to be saying the opposite.

In such times of doubt, we are called to fight for our faith by giving our questions and fears to the one who truly knows the answers — God. This may require us to let go of our need for validation and closure or our desire to know what the future holds. While it may be challenging, the cost is worth it, as there is no safer place to carry our doubts than in God's hands. He will give us His peace in return, providing us with the strength and confidence to keep moving forward in faith (see Philippians 4:6-7).

The Serpent is Everywhere

The serpent manifests itself in various forms and methods in our lives today. It can come through the media we consume, the negative thoughts that plague us during difficult times, or even through the influence of friends and family who may try to lead us away from God's path. They may try to sow seeds of doubt in our minds, questioning God's commands and making us feel like we are missing out by following Jesus instead of conforming to the world's ways. Unlike when Eve fell into temptation, we must resist the serpent's deceitfulness and not give in to sin, which leads to spiritual death and separation from God. Instead, we should be inspired by David, who desired to understand and follow God's commands out of reverence for His goodness. David recognized God's goodness and wrote, "You are good and do only good; teach me your decrees" (Psalm 119:68). Therefore, hold firm to your faith, trust God and obey His commands.

SEE THE STORY IN GENESIS 2:4-3:24, 3:1-24

A THREAD OF FAITH

When we walk with the Lord
In the light of His Word,
What a glory He sheds on our way;
While we do His good will,
He abides with us still,
And with all who will trust and obey.
Trust and obey,
For there's no other way
To be happy in Jesus,
But to trust and obey.

Not a shadow can rise,
Not a cloud in the skies,
But His smile quickly drives it away;
Not a doubt or a fear,
Not a sigh or a tear,
Can abide while we trust and obey.

Not a burden we bear,
Not a sorrow we share,
But our toil He doth richly repay;
Not a grief or a loss,
Not a frown or a cross,
But is blest if we trust and obey.

But we never can prove

A THREAD OF FAITH

The delights of His love,
Until all on the altar we lay;
For the favor He shows,
And the joy He bestows,
Are for them who will trust and obey.

Then in fellowship sweet
We will sit at His feet,
Or we'll walk by His side in the way;
What He says we will do;
Where He sends, we will go,
Never fear, only trust and obey.

Hymn by John H. Sammis (1846–1919)

2

THE FAITH OF SARAH

Sarai and Abram, a married couple in ancient times, faced the heart-wrenching challenge of infertility for many years. As Sarai advanced in age, the realization that her chances of bearing children were diminishing took a heavy toll on her. In her society, the ability to bear children held great significance for a woman's identity, which added to Sarai's emotional burden. One day, Abram had a significant encounter when God appeared to him and promised that he would have a descendant and that his offspring would be as plentiful as the stars in the sky (see Genesis 15:4-6). Despite this promise, Sarai, eager to have a child, offered her servant Hagar to her husband in a genuine effort to fulfill her desire for motherhood, and Abram agreed.

Sarai's Desperation

Sarai grappled with an incredibly heart-wrenching decision when she offered her servant to her husband. The intense, all-consuming longing to become a mother had plagued her for so long that she saw this as her only chance to realize her dream, even if it meant disregarding the promise God made to her husband. This decision caused her profound pain as Sarai had to witness the man she loved marrying someone else and having a child with them. One can't help but wonder if Sarai often found herself in tears, imagining the life she could have had if only she could conceive a child. The situation was further complicated by Sarai's mistreatment of Hagar, stemming from her belief that Hagar looked down on her. Sarai's jealousy and bitterness toward Hagar may have intensified as Hagar's pregnancy progressed, which served as a constant reminder to Sarai of her inability to conceive.

God's Promise to Sarai

After Hagar gave birth to a son named Ishmael, thirteen years later, God appeared to Abram again (see Genesis 17). During this encounter, God made a significant promise to Abram and entered into a covenant with him. God stated that Abram would be the father of many nations and that kings would come from him. Abram was 99 years old, and his wife Sarai was 90, far beyond her childbearing years. Despite their old age and initial rebellion against God's first promise, God was faithful and gave them another promise and changed their names to reflect it. Initially known as Abram, God changed his name to Abraham, which means "father of nations." This renaming symbolized the fulfillment of God's promise to make him the father of many nations.

Similarly, God changed Sarai's name to Sarah, which means "princess." God blessed Sarah, promising she would become a royal princess, a mother of nations and kings. Initially, when God made this promise to Sarah and Abraham, they found it challenging to believe. After years of praying without any sign of fulfillment, the idea seemed impossible. Sarah was advanced in age, and not only was she barren, but her faith and hope of conceiving had also faded away.

Faith Restored, and a Promise Fulfilled

Sarah's faith was restored by God when He promised her that she would become a mother and a mother to nations and kings. Initially, she struggled to believe it, but eventually, she entrusted herself to God's faithfulness.

Sarah witnessed the fulfillment of God's promise when she conceived and gave birth to a son named Isaac, which means "laughter." Sarah and Abraham had initially laughed in disbelief at the thought of having a child in their old age. However, when Isaac was born, Sarah was joyful and declared that God had brought her laughter. She also stated that everyone who heard about it would share her joy (see Genesis 21:6).

The delight she must have felt was immeasurable as Sarah laughed out loud, her aged body carrying God's promise, and her wrinkled hands cradling the child she had yearned for, for all those years. All the pain, confusion, and tears Sarah had endured over the years faded away at that moment. None of it mattered anymore because faith had once again burst forth as she embraced this incredible promise from God.

The Covenant

After Isaac grew up, God told Abraham to sacrifice him. This command must have felt very heavy for Abraham, and it must have been painful for him to think of the pain Sarah would feel of losing their child after waiting for so long to have him. However, despite the pain and weight of the command, Abraham obeyed and built an altar to sacrifice his beloved son. Just as Abraham was about to sacrifice his son, God stepped in and provided a ram instead (see Genesis 22). Because of Abraham's faith and obedience, God made a promise to him.

God promised Abraham that his descendants would multiply greatly and that his offspring would bring blessings to all nations on earth (see Genesis 18:22). Abraham and Sarah may not have fully understood when or how God would fulfill these promises, but they embraced them in faith. Little did they know, through their faith, that God had begun His story of redemption to reconcile all humanity to Himself.

The Role of the Faith of Sarah in God's Redemption Plan

Sarah lived an incredibly long life, reaching the age of 127. Despite not witnessing God's promise of becoming the mother of kings, she held onto her faith that this promise would come to fruition.

God eventually rewarded her belief when the royal line of King David descended from her, ultimately leading to the birth of Jesus Christ, the Savior.

According to Galatians 3:16, Jesus is referred to as the "offspring" of Abraham, highlighting the significance of Sarah's lineage.

By believing in Jesus Christ, people are saved from their sins and blessed with eternal life (see John 3:36). The disobedience and distrust displayed by Eve towards God resulted in the separation of humanity from God. However, the good news is that by believing in Jesus Christ, we attain salvation and reunite with God.

Although, Sarah initially had doubts, God remained faithful and restored her faith. Eventually, she became an important part of His redemption plan. Hebrews 11:11 praises her for trusting in God's faithfulness, which emphasizes our need for God and His promises during our struggles with faith.

Encouragement

"Now faith is confidence in what we hope for and assurance about what we do not see."

Hebrews 11:1

When we pray and wait for the fulfillment of our desires, there are moments when our faith may falter. We may become discouraged and tempted to take matters into our own hands, just as Sarah did. However, it is in these moments that God calls us to act differently. He encourages us to see beyond what our physical eyes can perceive and instead view the situation through the lens of faith.

Faith is not a blind or ignorant belief; instead, it provides the ability to see and comprehend. It enables us to perceive the unseen and trust in God's promises and in His will. When Sarah longed for a child and found her faith wavering, God's promises opened her eyes and renewed her faith. He reassured her of His faithfulness and guided her to trust Him.

Therefore, as we navigate through life's journey, we can find assurance and clarity in God's promises. When we take the time to reflect on His teachings and actively seek His wisdom, we become more attuned to His steadfast kindness and reliability in our lives. Even when His plans may seem unclear to us, we understand that His intentions are always for our ultimate good. This deep understanding fortifies our faith and empowers us to trust Him completely. By meditating on and holding onto God's promises, we can strengthen our faith in the unseen and trust that God is always at work, even when we can't see the outcome.

So, which promises do you need to seek from God's word to fortify your faith in the invisible? Allow them to serve as a wellspring of inspiration for you.

Nahum 1:7 - "The Lord is good, a refuge in times of trouble. He cares for those who trust in him."

> This promise reminds us that we can turn to God for help and support when we feel overwhelmed or lost. It also assures us that God cares for us when we trust in Him.

2 Thessalonians 3:3 - "But the Lord is faithful, and he will strengthen you and protect you from the evil one."

This promise is particularly comforting when our faith is weak, and we feel vulnerable to the temptations and trials of the world. It reminds us that we can rely on God's faithfulness to shield us and give us the strength to face any challenge.

Psalm 37:4 - "Take delight in the Lord, and he will give you the desires of your heart."

This promise reminds us that when we prioritize our relationship with God and seek His will above all else, He will provide for us according to His perfect timing. It encourages us to find joy and satisfaction in our relationship with God, knowing that He is faithful to keep His promises.

SEE THE STORY IN GENESIS 16:1-15; 17:1-27

3

THE FAITH OF REBEKAH

After Sarah passed away, Abraham was deeply concerned about finding a suitable wife for his son Isaac. He was determined that Isaac should not marry a Canaanite woman, as he wanted his son to marry someone from his own country. Abraham sent his trusted servant to their homeland to find a wife for Isaac. The servant was eager to fulfill his master's wishes but also worried about what would happen if he found a suitable woman who refused to return with him. Abraham assured the servant that

God would guide him and even send His angel to help him in his quest. He also clarified that the servant would be released from his oath if the woman refused to follow him.

Seeking a wife for Issac

The servant set out on his journey to Mesopotamia, the homeland of Abraham. Upon reaching his destination, he carefully positioned his camels near the well of water just outside the city. The evening had set in, the time when women traditionally came to draw water. Anticipating the unfolding events, the servant anxiously awaited the fulfillment of his master's wishes. He prayed to God for success and a sign, saying, "Lord, God of my master Abraham, please grant me success today and show kindness to my master. As I stand by this spring, the daughters of the townspeople will come to draw water. If I ask a young woman for a drink and she offers water to my camels, let her be the one for Isaac. This will be the sign that you have shown kindness to my master" (Genesis 24:42). Before he could finish his prayer, Rebekah was already approaching the springs to draw water.

Rebekah's Hospitality

Rebekah's evening took an unexpected turn as the sun dipped below the horizon and cast a warm glow over the landscape. I imagine her carefully approaching the ancient well with her worn pitcher. She skillfully drew water from the well, ensuring no precious drop was spilled. Every step she took was cautious, her eyes never leaving the task at hand, mindful of avoiding mishaps.

Amid this quiet ritual, her thoughts were suddenly interrupted by a polite voice. Abraham's servant, weary from his journey, respectfully requested, "Please let me drink." In an era where fetching water was complex and time-consuming, offering water to a stranger held deep significance. Rebekah, showing humility and compassion, graciously offered her pitcher to the servant, allowing him to quench his thirst despite the significant time and effort it took to draw the water. She didn't stop there. Rebekah went above and beyond, offering water to the servant's camels. Though seemingly ordinary to her, this act of kindness was a miraculous answer to the servant's prayer unfolding before his eyes.

The Servant's Prayer Answered

At that moment, the servant realized he had found a suitable wife for Isaac. This realization sparked curiosity within the servant's heart, and he asked Rebekah about her father's identity and if there was space for him to stay at her father's house for the night. As Rebekah revealed her father's name and her connection to Abraham, the servant felt a deep sense of reverence. He humbly bowed his head and worshiped the Lord, acknowledging God's divine guidance that had led him to his master's relatives. During that time, it was common for close relatives in Abraham's family to marry each other. Marriages between close relatives were not yet forbidden by

God (see Leviticus 18:6-18). So, it was not unusual for the servant to find a wife for Isaac within Abraham's family.

The Faith of Rebekah

When Rebekah heard the servant's words, she was filled with excitement. She hurriedly made her way to inform her family about Abraham's servant's arrival. The news sparked a buzz of anticipation as the family eagerly prepared to accommodate the servant and his camels for the night. Little did Rebekah know that this unexpected encounter would begin a profound and life-altering journey for her.

As the evening unfolded, the servant provided a captivating and detailed explanation for his visit, recounting the extraordinary story of Abraham and the challenges he had faced in his quest to find Rebekah and her family. I imagine the room was calm, and all the family's attention was fixed on the servant's heartfelt testimony, creating a moment of wonder. Rebekah's heart must have quickened with a mixture of emotions as she realized that her simple act of kindness had led to this momentous occasion.

Humbly, the servant then requested Rebekah's hand in marriage on behalf of his master's son. The family readily accepted his request without hesitation. Rebekah, too, accepted the proposal. Her faith and immediate acceptance of the servant's proposal shined through as a testament to her strong belief in God's will. Despite never seeing Isaac, she courageously agreed to marry him. Her determined response, "I will go," demonstrated her trust in God's plan.

Rebekah's courageous leap into the unknown ultimately led her to become Isaac's beloved wife, setting a remarkable journey that would shape history.

The Role of the Faith of Rebekah in God's Redemption Plan

Rebekah's kindness towards Abraham's servant and her faith in God paved the way for her to play a significant role in God's grand plan of redemption. God blessed Rebekah with the birth of twin sons, Esau and Jacob. Little did she know that, through Jacob, the twelve tribes of Israel would emerge, with one of those tribes being Judah. It was from the lineage of Judah that Jesus Christ, the Savior of humanity, and the promised offspring of Abraham would eventually come.

Through Jesus Christ, all people can find forgiveness for their sins and attain eternal life by placing their faith in Him. Rebekah's simple act of kindness and her faith in God had far-reaching consequences, ultimately leading to the salvation and redemption of humanity. Just as Rebekah became part of God's redemption plan through her faith and kindness, we, too, become part of His plans through our faith.

Encouragement

"But someone will say, 'you have faith; I have deeds.' Show me your faith without deeds, and I will show you my faith by my deeds." James 2:18

We must hold onto our faith in God and let it guide us toward showing hospitality to others, especially in a world that often glorifies self-centeredness. We must strive to be a beacon of light amidst the darkness surrounding us. Every day offers us numerous chances to bring glory to God, even in our most straightforward tasks. During these seemingly ordinary moments, God can reveal His extraordinary plans and purposes for us. By approaching each day with faith, humility, kindness, gentleness, and love, we open ourselves to the incredible ways God can use us. Sometimes, we may feel that our actions are insignificant, but like Rebekah, whose small act of kindness set her on a transformative journey of faith, our selfless service can pave the way for our faith to bear abundant fruit.

Therefore, we must not be discouraged by the everyday chores and responsibilities that lie ahead. Instead, we should embrace them as opportunities to showcase our faith and allow God to work through us. We must understand that even the most minor acts of service can have a profound impact on our own lives and the lives of those around us. Through these actions, we can spread love and kindness and ultimately participate in God's plans and purposes.

SEE THE STORY IN GENESIS 24

4

THE FAITH OF LEAH

Jacob, also known as Israel, was a man of deep emotions, and when he laid eyes on Rachel, his uncle Laban's daughter, he was instantly captivated. The intensity of his feelings overwhelmed him, causing him to kiss her and cry out in sheer joy. At that very moment, Jacob realized he had found the woman he wanted to spend the rest of his life with. However, Jacob soon discovered that marrying Rachel would be a challenging task. In those times, it was customary for the groom to present the bride's father with a significant sum of money, known as the bride price, as a gesture of respect and commitment. Not discouraged by the challenge, Jacob made a bold proposition to Laban — he offered to work for him for seven years in exchange for the equivalent value of Rachel's bride price.

Laban agreed to the arrangement, recognizing Jacob's determination and love for Rachel.

Jacob Works to Win Rachel

And so, Jacob embarked on a journey of hard work and dedication, toiling day and night under Laban's watchful eye. He poured his heart and soul into his work, driven to earn Rachel's hand in marriage. I imagine Jacob's affection for Rachel grew stronger during those seven years.

Perhaps he spent countless hours getting to know her, listening to her hopes and dreams, and sharing his own. He was determined to prove his worthiness and earn her love. However, Jacob's situation took an unexpected turn. Laban cleverly deceived Jacob on the wedding night by substituting Rachel with her older sister, Leah. When Jacob discovered the switch the following day, he likely felt shock, anger, and disappointment. He confronted Laban, demanding an explanation for this deceitful act. Laban justified his actions by stating that it was customary for the older sister to marry before the younger one.

Laban, with his cunning negotiation skills, proposed a solution to Jacob. He also suggested Jacob marry Rachel, but he would have to work for Laban for another seven years in exchange. Despite his situation, Jacob reluctantly agreed to this unexpected turn of events. He accepted Leah as his wife, but his heart still longed for Rachel. Despite the hardships and the unexpected twists of fate, Jacob's love for Rachel remained strong.

The Faith of Leah

Leah knew that Jacob's heart belonged to her younger sister, not her. The pain of being in a marriage where true love was absent must have been unimaginable. Leah must have constantly questioned why she was the least favored and pondered the countless reasons that prevented Jacob from loving her. However, God saw her suffering during her darkest moments and blessed her with the ability to conceive. I can only imagine the overwhelming joy Leah experienced when she discovered she was carrying Jacob's child, praying that the pregnancy would significantly change their marriage. As her belly grew, so did her hope for a loving and affectionate bond with her husband.

With her newborn son cradled in her arms, Leah's heart overflowed with gratitude and hope. She named her son Reuben, which means "behold, a son," symbolizing the transformation she longed for in her marriage. Leah believed this precious child would be the key to unlocking Jacob's heart and bridging their emotional gap.

Leah's heart overflowed with joy as she experienced the miracle of becoming pregnant again. This time, she lovingly named her newborn son Simeon, which signifies "to be heard." This precious child symbolized that the Lord had indeed listened to her prayers and granted her the gift of another child. Shortly after, Leah became pregnant for the third time and named her son Levi, meaning "joined." With certainty, she declared that her husband would now be attached to her, having given birth to three sons. In a remarkable turn of events, Leah became pregnant for the fourth time and named her son Judah, which translates to "praise." On this occasion, she expressed her intention to praise the Lord.

Despite the challenges of her loveless marriage and the constant temptation to resent her sister, Rachel, Leah chose a different path. She turned to God, placing her faith in Him. She firmly believed that God saw her, heard her, and ultimately blessed her.

The Role of Leah's Faith in God's Redemption Plan

Leah's story is about a woman who longed for love. Although her story initially focuses on her desire for love, her faith in God elevates her story to something more significant. God established the lineage leading to King David through her son

Judah.

King David was well-known for his strong connection with God and his role as a great leader. His bloodline ultimately leads to the birth of Jesus Christ, who embodies God's love and forgiveness. Like Leah, those who long for love discover a love that surpasses all understanding in Jesus Christ. By having faith in Jesus and His sacrifice on the cross, God forgives people of their sins, redeems them, and enter into a relationship that surpasses any earthly relationship — a relationship with God. By embracing Jesus, individuals find comfort, strength, and everlasting love that will never fade or disappoint.

Leah and Rachel went on to have more children, and God chose both to fulfill the promise He gave Abraham. This promise was about making Abraham the father of a great nation, (see Genesis 12:2-3).

Through Rachel and Leah's children the twelve children — the twelve tribes of Israel were formed by God, which became the foundation of the nation that would come from Abraham's family. Ultimately, Jesus Christ was born from this lineage, and God redeemed humanity through Him (see Colossians 1:12-14).

Encouragement

"Those who know your name trust in you, for you, Lord, have never forsaken those who seek you." Psalm 9:10

Despite facing rejection and feeling unloved by her husband, Jacob, Leah looked to God in faith. She found comfort and strength in her relationship with Him, knowing that only God can ease troubles.

By staying strong in our faith in Jesus, we, too, can find true freedom and love in Him. We can find a deep sense of belonging and value in His presence, believing He will never abandon us when we seek Him.

Just as Leah's pain and desires were part of God's

plan, our struggles and desires can also serve a greater purpose as we surrender them to God, allowing Him to turn them into something beautiful that brings glory to His name.

SEE THE STORY IN GENESIS 29 AND GENESIS 30

5

THE FAITH OF THE MIDWIVES

Joseph was one of Jacob's twelve sons. His father gifted him a coat of many colors, which made his brothers jealous. They sold him into slavery in Egypt (see Genesis 37:18-36), where his master's wife falsely accused him of a crime, leading to his imprisonment. Despite this, he interpreted the dreams of two fellow prisoners and impressed Pharaoh with his abilities. Pharaoh appointed him the second-in-command over all of Egypt after he interpreted Pharaoh's dreams, which foretold seven years of abundance followed by seven years of famine (see Genesis 41:1-36).

Israel's Journey to Egypt

As predicted by Joseph, the famine struck, and Jacob and his family heard about the abundance of food in Egypt. They recognized an opportunity for salvation and decided to travel to Egypt for refuge and sustenance under Joseph's care (see Genesis 46). Despite the emotional toll of leaving the land of Canaan, which held great significance for Jacob and his ancestors, they knew it was necessary for their survival.

God had promised Abraham and his descendants the land of Canaan as an everlasting possession (see Genesis 17:8). Although Jacob and his family were foreigners in Canaan, they knew they were part of God's promise to Abraham and would eventually return to the Promised Land (see Genesis 46:3-4).

Upon their arrival in Egypt, Joseph warmly welcomed Jacob and his family. Under Joseph's care, the Israelites thrived in their new home. He gave the Israelites fertile land to cultivate (see Genesis 47:11). Joseph provided for their physical needs and preserved their spiritual and cultural traditions. He allowed them to maintain their customs and faith in God, even in a foreign land.

Israelite Population Multiplied

As the Israelites multiplied in Egypt, their growing numbers became a testament to the faithfulness of God, each newborn child serving as a reminder of God's promise to Abraham. It was a promise that he would become the father of a great nation that God had chosen for a specific purpose. This nation was to be as numerous as the stars in the sky and the sand on the seashore. As the Israelites continued to multiply, they carried the hope and expectation of becoming a great nation that would bring forth the promised offspring. This offspring would bless all the earth's nations, fulfilling God's covenant with Abraham (see Genesis 22:17-18).

A New King Rules Egypt

A new ruler took the throne in Egypt and

disregarded Joseph's contributions and influence after the deaths of Jacob, Joseph, and his brothers. Over time, the king became increasingly worried about the growing population of the Israelites. He believed their increasing numbers could lead to a rebellion or war. Fearing that the Israelites might join forces with their enemies and revolt against him, the king made a drastic decision. He enslaved the Israelites and made their lives in Egypt extremely difficult (see Exodus 1:8-11).

The king sought to wipe out God's chosen people by any means necessary. To address the perceived threat, he gave a chilling order to the midwives, commanding them to kill all male infants born to the Israelites (see Exodus 1:16). The midwives were experts in helping women during childbirth. They supported women during labor, cut the baby's umbilical cord, bathed the newborn, and introduced the baby to the parents.

The Midwives' Reverence for God

I envision the midwives cradling the babies in their arms, the babies' cries echoing through the air, while the midwives remembered the king's decree to end their lives. They observed these newborns' delicate hands and feet and experienced the miracle of their first breaths as they gently embraced their tiny forms. How could they ever bring themselves to commit such an unthinkable act? It wasn't merely infants they cradled, but the embodiment of God's covenant with Abraham. As the two midwives held the newborn baby boys, their hearts raced with anxiety.

They knew that the decision they were about to make would have immense significance, not just for the babies but for themselves. Their fear was rooted in the knowledge of their ruthless ruler's relentless nature, and they dreaded the consequences of disobeying him. Yet, a more profound fear gripped their souls — the fear of God. At that moment, the midwives became a part of God's plan, which would have far-reaching consequences.

The Faith of the Midwives

Shiphrah and Puah disobeyed the king's orders.

THE FAITH OF THE MIDWIVES

They saved the lives of newborn boys, carefully planning for each birth they attended. I imagine how Shiphrah and Puah must have felt as they made their way to the Israelite women's homes, consumed by fear and determination. Their mission was urgent, requiring quick and efficient delivery of newborn babies, while ensuring their safety and avoiding any suspicion from the authorities. The once joyful profession of these two midwives had now turned into a dangerous mission of secrecy, where every move had to be carefully calculated to protect the lives of innocent infants. It was a battle of good and evil, with Shiphrah and Puah on the front lines, fighting to preserve the sanctity of life against all odds.

Perhaps the midwives constantly scanned the horizon for any sign of the king's officials, filling their days with a sense of danger. They knew one misstep could mean their deaths, but their mission was too important to abandon. They were driven by a deep sense of fear and faith in God, giving them the strength to carry on. Their bravery and rebellion against the cruel orders of the king played a vital role in fulfilling God's promise to Abraham.

The Role of the Midwives' Faith in God's Redemption Plan

In Genesis 12:2-3, God promised Abraham that he would become the father of a great nation and bless all families of the earth through him. The growth and strength of his descendants were essential in fulfilling this promise.

When the midwives disobeyed the king's orders to kill the Hebrew babies, they ensured that the Israelite population continued to thrive. By doing so, they prevented the Israelites from being wiped out and helped them flourish. This act of rebellion and kindness had a profound impact on all of humanity, as it set off a chain of events that led to the birth of Jesus Christ, the promised descendant of Abraham who would bless all nations of the earth (see Galatians 3:16). Jesus was born into the Israelite lineage and came to fulfill God's promise of that blessing. Through faith in Jesus Christ, people are saved, forgiven of their sins, and given eternal life with God (see Ephesians 2:8-9). The impact of the midwives' actions extended far beyond their own lives, paving the way for God's plan for redemption.

Encouragement

"Let us run with perseverance the race marked out for us, fixing our eyes on Jesus, the pioneer and perfecter of faith." Hebrews 12:1-2

The midwives' story reminds us that our faith in God should not be limited to words and beliefs. We must demonstrate it through our actions and decisions. Even when we face challenges and temptations, we should stay committed to God and His principles. Giving in to fear and compromising our faith is easy in a world full of darkness and uncertainty. However, the midwives' story teaches us that true transformation and redemption come from standing firm in our beliefs, even during difficult times. By living out our faith and allowing others to see its power, we can bring about change in our homes and communities. Our obedience to God can profoundly impact those around us, leading to unexpected and amazing results. When we stand firm in our faith and obey God, we open ourselves to His blessings and intervention.

Our faith becomes a catalyst for miracles and breakthroughs beyond our understanding. We become an essential part of God's plan for redemption, playing a crucial role in bringing His kingdom to earth.

Therefore, let's not just talk about our faith in God. Instead, let's strive to live it out in every aspect of our lives. Let's stay strong in the face of darkness or persecution and allow the world to see the incredible results of our faith and obedience to God. By doing so, we become like a thread God can use to weave His plans and purposes into the world.

SEE THE STORY IN EXODUS 1:15-21

6

THE FAITH OF JOCHEBED

The attempt to eliminate Israelite baby boys right after birth was unsuccessful, so the Pharaoh devised a new plan. This time, he ordered that all male children born to the Hebrews should be thrown into the river Nile (see Exodus 1:22). When the Egyptian king commanded his soldiers to seize all Israelite baby boys, Jochebed became terrified. She understood that her son was in danger, and she was determined to safeguard him at any cost.

The Faith of Jochebed

Despite being commanded and intimidated by the

king, Jochebed displayed remarkable courage and love for her child. With a heart overflowing with affection and faith in God, she went to great lengths to safeguard her precious baby. I can only imagine the countless sleepless nights she endured, keeping a watchful eye over her child, offering up fervent prayers for his well-being, and trusting in God's ultimate plan. As the tension and fear in the land grew, her love for her son grew stronger, and she remained determined to shield him from harm.

The day arrived when she had to confront the truth that she could no longer keep her beloved child hidden. Instead of giving in to despair and allowing her baby to meet an untimely end, her faith grew even stronger. In a desperate move, Jochebed, carefully placed her son in a basket and gently released him into the flowing waters of the Nile River. As she watched the basket drift away, one can only imagine the heaviness in her heart and the tears welling up in her eyes. Although no one witnessed the torment tearing her heart apart, God saw the faith that filled it.

Jochebed's Faith Rewarded

As Jochebed watched the basket disappear into the silent Nile River, her heart must have been heavy with sorrow. But she needed to let her son go and only trust that God would protect her son. Meanwhile, her older daughter, Miriam (see Numbers 26:59), stood at a distance and watched the basket, hoping for her brother's safety. Suddenly, a figure appeared in the distance. It was Pharaoh's daughter, who had come to the river for her daily bath. As she drew closer, she noticed the basket floating in the water. Her heart filled with compassion as she opened the lid and saw the beautiful baby boy inside; she desired to adopt him. At that moment, Miriam rushed forward, introducing herself as a Hebrew girl and offering Jochebed to nurse the baby.

Miriam's kindness moved the Pharaoh's daughter, who agreed to let Jochebed, the baby's mother, nurse and care for him. Jochebed must have felt overwhelmed with gratitude and joy as she saw God's mercy and love in this miraculous turn of events. God mended her heart, and she knew He had shown up for her and her family in their time of need. Jochebed had surrendered her baby boy to God, trusting that He would keep him safe. Indeed, through God's providence, not only was her baby boy kept secure, but she could also nurse him without any hindrance, and she even received compensation for it.

The Role of Jochebed's Faith in God's Redemption Plan

The Pharaoh's daughter named Jochebed's son Moses. Jochebed had no idea that the child she protected and entrusted to God would play a crucial role in God's plan for redemption. God chose Moses to lead the Israelites out of slavery and into the land God promised to Abraham. Through their journey from bondage to freedom, the Israelites experienced God's redemption, salvation, and blessings.

Jochebed's faith was instrumental in the salvation of God's people, paving the way for Jesus Christ, the ultimate Savior, to bring redemption to all. Her example shows that one does not need to be extraordinary to fulfill God's plans; faith and obedience to do what's right before God are key.

Encouragement

"Trust in the LORD with all your heart and lean not on your understanding; in all your ways submit to him, and he will make your paths straight." Proverbs 3:5-6

In a world where wickedness seems to be increasing daily, it's often difficult to find a source of inspiration to help us navigate the chaos. However, we can take inspiration from Jochebed, who demonstrated faith in God amid darkness and wickedness. She did not surrender to the government's laws that contradicted God's ways but trusted God's ability to provide a way out of the situation. As mothers, we can learn from Jochebed's example and greatly shield our children from the corrupting influences of media, culture, and an ungodly education system. We can ensure the safety and well-being of our children by consistently teaching them the principles and teachings found in God's word. By instilling these truths and commandments in their hearts, we can provide them with a strong moral foundation to guide them through life's challenges. We can have faith that, no matter the obstacles we face, God will always provide us with the strength and wisdom to protect and nurture our children.

We may worry about our children when they grow up and are no longer under our care and protection. But we can rest assured that God will watch over them. As He watched over baby Moses in the river Nile, we can confidently release them into His loving hands. By nurturing our children physically and spiritually, and by instilling in them the Word of God, we can have faith that God will use their faith to bring others to the saving grace of Jesus Christ. Our faith in God can position us to play a part in God's plan of redemption.

Therefore, let us not be afraid to take a stand for what we believe in, even if it goes against the norms of society. Let us steadfastly believe in God, knowing He will never leave or forsake us (see Deuteronomy 31:8). And let us trust in God's ability to provide a way out of any situation, no matter how difficult it may seem. With God on our side, we can overcome any obstacle and play our part in God's plan for redemption.

SEE THE STORY IN EXODUS 2:1-10 AND EXODUS 6:20, NUMBERS 26:59

A THREAD OF FAITH

7

THE FAITH OF ZIPPORAH

When Moses had grown up in the palace of Pharaoh, he witnessed Egyptians violently attacking a Hebrew slave. Out of a strong sense of justice and compassion for his fellow man, he intervened and ended up killing the aggressor. Fearing the consequences of his actions, he had to bury the deceased quickly to avoid detection. Eventually, Pharaoh discovered this incident, which prompted him to take action against Moses. With his life in immediate danger, Moses had no other option but to escape to the faraway land of Midian, leaving behind his life of privilege in Egypt. In this unfamiliar territory, specifically at a well, he crossed paths with Zipporah, the daughter of the priest of Midian, who would eventually become his wife.

God's Calling to Moses

Moses found love and companionship in Zipporah during his stay in Midian. Their bond was blessed by God, and they were given two sons. However, their peaceful life was soon interrupted by an unexpected revelation. One day, Moses experienced the divine presence of the Lord, who urged him to return to Egypt and lead the Israelites to freedom. This mission was of utmost importance, and Moses had no choice but to return to where he had fled and take on this vital mission.

The Faith of Zipporah

The call from God disrupted Moses' life and that of his wife, Zipporah. Imagine the shock and disbelief that must have overcome her as she heard what the Lord had asked of her husband. The task at hand was to free a people whom the Egyptians had enslaved for 400 years. Zipporah must have been overwhelmed to comprehend how God would make it happen. However, despite not knowing how God would use her husband to end centuries of slavery, Zipporah summoned all the courage and faith she had and supported him.

The decision to support her husband must have been difficult for her, as she would be left alone with their children while Moses took on this dangerous and challenging mission. Her trust in God and love for her husband gave her the strength to leave everything behind. She believed God called Moses to do something great and ensured she was by his side in the mission.

Together, they embarked on a journey filled with uncertainties and challenges, holding on to nothing but God's word and instructions. Riding on a donkey with their two sons, they left behind their familiar surroundings and cherished home, venturing into the unknown. After a long and challenging journey, they finally arrived at a lodging place, where an unexpected event took place — God revealed His intention to kill Moses. The method through which God intended to carry out this plan remains a mystery.

The Role of Zipporah's Faith in God's Redemption Plan

In a moment of swift action, Zipporah realized the gravity of the situation; she took a sharp stone and circumcised her son, throwing the foreskin at Moses' feet. Through her quick thinking and bravery, she saved her husband's life. Imagine the immense courage she displayed in that moment, as the baby's cries echoed through the air, piercing the silence. Despite the brutality and bloodshed involved, Zipporah's act of circumcising their son demonstrated her faith in following God's laws.

Moses, an Israelite belonging to the tribe of Levi, had a special connection to God through the covenant made with his ancestor Abraham. Being aware of this covenant, Zipporah remembered that every male child must be circumcised when they reach eight days old. Furthermore, any male who remained uncircumcised would be excluded from their community, as they would have violated God's covenant (see Genesis 17:10–14).

Moses stayed in Midian for a long time and forgot to follow God's covenant with his ancestors. Perhaps this was a reminder from God to Moses about the covenant and his true identity as a Hebrew before he could lead the Israelites to freedom from slavery. Although we don't know the exact reason why God tried to kill Moses, we do know that circumcision ultimately saved his life. Zipporah's faith and bravery in upholding the covenant played a role in God sparing Moses' life.

As stated above, after Zipporah performed the circumcision on their son; she took the bloody foreskin and placed it on Moses' feet, exclaiming, "Surely you are a bridegroom of blood to me!" This act symbolized the covenant between Moses and God, as the blood circumcision was a sign that the Israelites belonged to God. The sign of blood was later placed on doorposts during the Passover, and it was another powerful symbol of this covenant (see

Exodus 12:13). Without Zipporah's bravery and faith, Moses may not have survived to continue his journey toward redeeming God's people from slavery. Therefore, Zipporah became an essential part of God's plan for redemption, demonstrating how our faith can make us an integral part of God's plans and purposes.

Encouragement

> *"All are justified freely by his grace through the redemption that came by Christ Jesus. God presented Christ as a sacrifice of atonement, through the shedding of his blood—to be received by faith:" Romans 3:24-25*

Bridegroom of Blood

Zipporah's mention of the "bridegroom of blood" foreshadowed the coming of the ultimate Bridegroom of blood, who would ultimately save the world from sin, death, and damnation. Just as

Moses and the Israelites were bound to God through blood, we are now united with God through Jesus' blood by placing our faith in Him and His sacrifice on the cross. Zipporah's willingness to enter into the covenant of circumcision shielded her husband from God's wrath, mirroring how God redeems us through the covenant of Jesus Christ's death and resurrection.

Share the Gospel and Intercede.

In a world filled with countless distractions and temptations, it becomes increasingly important to remain steadfast in our faith and to actively share the gospel with our loved ones. By sharing the Gospel, we have the opportunity to lead our families toward establishing a covenant relationship with God, allowing them to experience the life-changing power of faith in Jesus' death and resurrection. Zipporah's obedience and faith in God's covenant brought about the salvation of her husband. Similarly, through our prayers and proclamation of the gospel, we can pave the way for the salvation of our own families.

Just as Zipporah took immediate action to intercede for her husband, Moses, we should also be prompt in offering intercessory prayers for our loved ones and diligently sharing the Gospel with them. It's important to boldly and confidently proclaim the Gospel, understanding that our words and actions have the potential to guide our loved ones into a covenant relationship with God, ultimately saving them from eternal separation from God in Hell. It's important not to underestimate the profound impact that our faith and obedience can have on the eternal destinies of those we care about. Therefore, let's be diligent in our prayers and intentional in sharing the message of hope and salvation with those around us.

SEE THE STORY IN EXODUS 2:15-22; EXODUS 4:24-26

8

THE FAITH OF RAHAB

After Moses's death, God had to select a new leader to guide the Israelites into the land that He had promised to their forefathers. God chose Joshua, who was from the tribe of Ephraim, to lead His people into the Promised Land (see Deuteronomy 31:7-8). The Israelites were to first cross through the city of Jericho before they could occupy the Promised Land. Joshua sent two spies to inspect the land in that city before they could conquer it (see Joshua 2:1).

Rahab Shields the Spies

As a group of spies embarked on their secret mission to explore the city of Jericho in Canaan, they stumbled upon the home of Rahab, a woman who was known to the people as a prostitute. However, her reputation did not define her entirely; she was a woman of great faith and respect for the Lord.

As soon as she discovered the presence of the spies in her house, she realized the danger they were in and took quick action to protect them. News of the arrival of spies in the city reached the king's ears, and he immediately dispatched his men to capture them. However, amidst the chaos and confusion, Rahab came to their aid. She immediately devised a plan to hide the spies on her roof.

As the king's men arrived, she cunningly deceived them by pretending not to know the spie's whereabouts. Rahab was well aware of the risks of shielding the spies, but she was determined to protect them at all costs. She knew that the Israelites had come to Jericho for a reason and that the fate of her city hung in the balance. Despite her fears and the danger she faced, Rahab believed that God had already granted the Israelites victory over Jericho.

The Faith of Rahab

On the rooftop of her home, Rahab approached the spies sent by Joshua. Despite the danger that her actions posed to her life, she shared her knowledge with them, hoping that it would secure her safety and that of her family. With deep faith in the power of God, Rahab fearlessly recounted the fear that had gripped the people of Jericho and how they had heard of the Israelites' miraculous escape from Egypt and their victories over two kings on their journey to the Promised Land. Her confidence in God's ability to protect and deliver the Israelites shone through her words as she recounted His mighty works and her understanding of His character. Rahab's courage and conviction were a testament to her faith in the God of Israel.

THE FAITH OF RAHAB

The Role of Rahab's Faith in God's Redemption Plan

Rahab's story is remarkable and filled with courage, faith, and redemption. Despite living under the laws and authority of the king of Jericho, Rahab boldly decided to align herself with God and defy the king's authority. Her heart was filled with faith in God, even as fear gripped the city. When the spies arrived at her doorstep, she expressed her trust and loyalty to God, instead of responding with hatred towards them. Her faith was evident when she boldly declared, "For the Lord your God, he is God in heaven above and earth beneath," (Joshua 2:8).

Rahab knew only God would spare her life from the coming destruction of the city. She put her trust in God's mercy and begged the spies to spare her life and that of her father's household. Through her kindness and faith, the spies promised to spare her life and that of her family. Rahab's faith and courage led to her salvation and that of her family, making her a part of God's redemption.

The story of Rahab is a powerful testament to the transformative power of faith. Once a sinful woman and an enemy of the God of Israel, Rahab's belief in

God allowed her to play a vital role in His plan for redemption. Her faith opened doors that she never thought possible when she married Salom, a respected leader of the tribe of Judah. This tribe, with its divine lineage, would eventually pave the way for the birth of Jesus Christ, the glorious offspring of Abraham (see Galatians 3:16).

Through Jesus Christ, individuals find salvation from their sins and receive the extraordinary gift of eternal life (see John 5:24).

Rahab's journey from sin to becoming a part of Jesus's lineage continues to captivate and inspire people today. Hebrews 11:31 commends her faith, showing the positive effects of faith in God.

Encouragement

"Believe in the Lord Jesus, and you will be saved, you and your household." Acts 16:31

Receiving God's limitless mercy by trusting Jesus Christ despite our past wrongdoings and

THE FAITH OF RAHAB

unworthiness is powerful and humbling. The story of Rahab serves as a reminder that faith can pave the way for redemption and salvation. Believers can attain salvation only by putting their faith in Jesus. The power of faith can influence those around us and help non-believers come to know Jesus Christ as their Savior and put their trust in Him.

Like Rahab, as we fervently seek God's salvation for ourselves, we should also intercede for the salvation of our loved ones. If we find ourselves lacking faith, we should earnestly ask God to grant us the faith to recognize our sinful nature and our need for salvation through Jesus Christ. We should also pray fervently for our families who need faith and are heading towards eternal damnation. We should ask God to open their eyes to their sinful state and the need for salvation.

SEE THE STORY IN JOSHUA 2-6

A THREAD OF FAITH

9

THE FAITH OF DEBORAH

After the death of Joshua, the respected leader of Israel, the Israelites turned their backs on God, abandoning their faith and instead worshiping idols and engaging in wicked deeds. This rebellion was a particularly grievous betrayal, given that God had previously rescued the Israelites from slavery in Egypt and had fulfilled His promise to their ancestors by giving them the land of Canaan, which they had settled in and made their home. However, despite being commanded to destroy the altars of the people already living in Canaan, the Israelites instead chose to embrace the Canaanite gods, leading to their disobedience and consequent punishment. As a result, God allowed neighboring nations to rule over them harshly, subjecting them to great suffering and oppression.

Despite their unfaithfulness, God showed the Israelites mercy by appointing Judges to save them from the consequences of their actions (see Judges 2:1-3). One such Judge was Deborah, who rose to prominence and became renowned for her wisdom and bravery in adversity.

The period of the judges in ancient Israel was a time of great political turmoil and instability. God chose a series of leaders who delivered the Israelites from oppression and established tenuous peace throughout the land during this era. The Judges played a crucial role in the military, defending the tribes of Israel against their enemies and ensuring their survival. During the reign of Jabin, the King of Canaan, the Israelites committed evil acts that resulted in their oppression. In their time of distress, they called upon God for help, and Deborah, a remarkable female Judge and prophetess, was chosen to lead and guide them.

The Unique Qualities that Set Deborah Apart as a Judge

Each Judge played a significant role in the wars and conflicts that plagued Israel during their time. Othniel, one of the Judges who preceded her, was known for his bravery and commitment to God's will. He led his people to many victories on the battlefield, earning him the title of "judge" in Israel. Ehud, on the other hand, was famous for his cleverness and resourcefulness. He was left-handed, which made him an unexpected and formidable opponent in battle. He crafted a sword with his hands and used it to rescue Israel from its enemies.

Every Judge in ancient Israel had their way of fulfilling God's purpose, but Deborah stood out among them all. Her faith and obedience to God became her weapons of warfare. As a prophetess, she possessed a unique gift crucial to God's plan. God entrusted her with a message for Barak, the military leader, and Deborah fearlessly delivered it.

The Faith of Deborah

Deborah informed Barak of God's plan to rescue Israel from the Canaanite army led by Sisera, King Jabin's forces commander. Deborah's faith shone through as they prepared for the battle, inspiring and encouraging Barak. With confidence and conviction, she assured him that the Lord would deliver Sisera into their hands. Her role in the war was crucial, as she provided spiritual guidance and strategic advice based on her prophetic insights.

Her words conveyed certainty and conviction that inspired Barak and the entire army. As Barak listened to the prophecy, I imagine he felt faith ignite in his heart and envisioned the end of 20 years of oppression under King Jabin's reign. While Barak was likely encouraged to go to war, Deborah's faith compelled him to ask her to accompany him. Deborah fearlessly agreed to accompany Barak, knowing God's hand was upon them. With Deborah by his side, Barak led the Israelites into battle, fully trusting God's plan.

As the battle unfolded, Deborah's prophecy proved to be true. The Lord intervened and confused Sisera's army, ultimately defeating them. Barak and his troops chased after the Canaanites and emerged victorious. However, Jael, a woman, played a crucial role in fulfilling another part of Deborah's prophecy. She killed Sisera, the commander, bringing an end to Jabin's reign and ushering in 40 years of peace for the people of Israel.

The Role of Deborah's Faith in God's Redemption Plan

Deborah didn't need to be as strong as Othniel or wield a sword like Ehud to be chosen by God to lead the Israelites out of oppression. Instead, her faith and obedience to God during a challenging time proved enough.

Deborah's faith was not only strong but also evident, yet she possessed a quiet quality within her faith that made her a unique leader who contributed to Israel's victory. Her respect and acknowledgment of Barak as the military leader were a testament to her character. Rather than diminishing his role, she utilized her faith to uplift and support him in his position. Her faith, humility and obedience allowed her to be part of God's plan to redeem the Israelites from oppression.

Encouragement

"Take up the shield of faith, with which you can extinguish all the flaming arrows of the evil one." Ephesians 6:16

Deborah is a compelling example for Christian women as she teaches much about faith, leadership, and overcoming adversity. Her story shows us that we do not need physical weapons in our war against the enemy. Instead, we can use our faith and relationship with God as weapons of warfare.

One key lesson we can learn from Deborah is respecting the authority of our husbands, pastors, and fathers. Even if we possess insights they may not have, we should use our faith to uplift and encourage them to excel in their roles. Acting this way requires a deep trust in God and a willingness to put our needs and desires aside to serve a higher purpose. At the same time, we can also use our unique insights and relationship with God to inspire and motivate the leaders in our lives.

This may involve offering them spiritual guidance, praying for them, and showing our support, as well as respectfully sharing our perspectives. By doing this, we can help them to become better leaders and contribute to the overall welfare of our communities.

Just as Barak led the army and wielded the sword, Deborah carried the faith that guided and strengthened them both. She used her unique insights and faith in God to encourage and inspire Barak, ultimately leading to their victory over their enemies.

SEE THE STORY IN JUDGES 3; JUDGES 4; JUDGES 5

10

THE FAITH OF MANOAH'S WIFE

In the times when judges held power in Israel, there lived a woman whose name remains unknown. She was married to a man named Manoah, and she could not conceive children. One day, to her great surprise, an angel of God appeared before her and delivered a message that would change her life forever. The angel told her she would bear a son, a unique child God chose. The angel gave the woman specific instructions on how to care for her child. She was to avoid drinking wine or strong drinks and anything unclean or impure. She was to follow the instructions because her child would be a Nazarite, dedicated to God from birth. The Nazarites were a unique group of people whom God set apart for the holy purpose of serving Him. They were forbidden from cutting their hair or drinking wine and were required to live a life of purity and devotion to God (see Numbers 6:1- 8).

The Promised Child

Upon hearing the incredible news of the promise of a child, Manoah's wife's heart was filled with excitement and anticipation. She wasted no time rushing to her husband to share every detail of her encounter with the angel. As she ran towards him, her heart must have raced as if it could leap out of her chest at any moment. She replayed the profound moment in her mind and shared every detail with her husband. Her husband listened intently, fully understanding the weight of the promise made to them.

Therefore, Manoah sought guidance from God on

how to raise this extraordinary child. He prayed fervently, beseeching God to send the angel he thought was the man of God to return and teach them how to nurture and guide their future son. God answered Manoah's prayer, and the angel appeared before Manoah's wife again. She hurriedly called her husband, and the angel confirmed everything his wife had shared with him about raising the promised child.

Overwhelmed with gratitude upon hearing the good news, Manoah offered the angel of the Lord to stay and suggested that they prepare a meal for him. This gesture was perhaps a way to honor the angel, whom they believed to be a man of God. However, instead of accepting the meal, the angel of the Lord proposed an alternative: a burnt offering as a sacrifice to God.

The Faith of Manoah's Wife

Manoah followed the angel's suggestion and offered a burnt sacrifice to God. After Manoah performed the sacrifice, the flames from the altar rose towards the heavens, creating a fiery blaze. As the fire ascended, the angel of the Lord ascended within them, leaving Manoah and his wife in awe. They realized that God had sent His angel as a messenger to them. Overwhelmed by disbelief and amazement, they fell prostrate on the ground, their faces touching the earth. Manoah trembled with fear, worried that he and his wife would die after having such an encounter. However, Manoah's wife was filled with faith and believed that God would not make a promise and accept their burnt offering only to bring harm upon them. She remained confident that God would fulfill His word and grant them a son.

The Role of Manoah's wife's Faith in God's Plan of Redemption

True to her faith, she gave birth to a son named Samson, whom God blessed abundantly as he grew. Later, God appointed Samson as the twelfth Judge of Israel to redeem them from the oppressive rule of the Philistines. Despite living an unfaithful life before God, Samson possessed incredible strength and often fought against the Philistines alone. Nevertheless, God remained faithful to His promise and used Samson to deliver Israel (see Judges 15:14-17). God rewarded Manoah's wife's faith in His ability to fulfill His promises when everything she hoped for came to fruition.

Encouragement

"He is not afraid of bad news; his heart is firm, trusting in the Lord." Psalm 112:7

The story of Manoah's wife is about a woman who had faith in God's promises, even when they seemed impossible. Despite being infertile, an angel assured her that she would have a son who would save Israel. Rather than doubting, she trusted God's plan and encouraged her husband to do the same. We can learn from her and be a voice of reason in a world full of doubt. By sharing stories of God's faithfulness, we remind others that He always keeps His word. Reflecting on our experiences, we can testify to His faithfulness, strengthening our faith and encouraging others.

Therefore, let us encourage others to trust God's promises and remind them that He always fulfills His word. By reminding ourselves and others of God's faithfulness, we can strengthen their faith and bring them peace and security. We can be a source of hope in a world of broken promises.

SEE THE STORY IN JUDGES 13

11

THE FAITH OF RUTH

During a time when the judges held authority over the land, a severe famine hit Bethlehem, leaving its inhabitants in a state of desperation. Naomi, her husband, and their two sons were among those who struggled to find sustenance and security amid this situation. To escape the famine's devastating effects, they decided to leave their homeland and seek refuge in the land of Moab, known for its abundance and prosperity.

Naomi's husband died, leaving her a widow with two young sons and shattering their hopes for a

THE FAITH OF RUTH

better life. Despite the challenges they faced, Naomi did her best to move forward, but tragedy struck again when both of her sons also passed away, leaving her with only her daughters-in-law, Orpah and Ruth. Naomi and her daughters-in-law were left in a desperate situation, struggling to make ends meet with no male relatives to provide for them. However, their fortunes began to change when Naomi received news that the Lord had once again provided food in her homeland of Bethlehem.

Naomi's Desire to Return Home

Naomi found a glimmer of hope in her homeland and yearned to return. She knew she couldn't provide for her daughters-in-law, so she urged them to return to their families. With a heavy heart, Naomi prayed to God for the kindness her daughters inlaw had shown her, her husband, and her sons to be reciprocated. She prayed to the Almighty to bless Orpah and Ruth with loving husbands who would provide them with security and stability. This prayer wasn't easy for Naomi, who had likely once envisioned a future filled with her husband's presence and the joy of having grandchildren. However, life had taken an unexpected turn, and her dreams and aspirations were shattered.

Naomi had spent many years in a foreign land, and as she prepared to leave and return to her homeland, her heart was heavy with grief and despair. Her daughters-in-law, who had become dear to her during their time together, begged her to allow them to accompany her. But Naomi knew she had nothing to offer them regarding security or support. As they embraced one another, tears streaming down their faces, they found comfort in each other's company. They were now bound not only by their familiarity with one another but also by the deep wounds they carried as widows, robbed of the bright futures they once envisioned.

Ruth's Commitment to Naomi

After bidding her mother-in-law Naomi a tearful farewell, Orpah departed, leaving Ruth behind to face the uncertain future. Naomi then advised Ruth to follow in Orpah's footsteps and return to her people and gods, knowing the hardships they had already encountered and the challenges ahead. However, Ruth refused to leave Naomi's side; her devotion and dedication shined through in her heartfelt words. Despite the adversity and pain they had endured, she professed her undying love and loyalty to Naomi. Ruth vowed to accompany Naomi wherever she went and reside wherever she chose to settle, even if that meant leaving behind everything she knew. She went so far as to declare that Naomi's community would become her own and Naomi's God would become her own, a testament to her commitment.

The Faith of Ruth

Ruth, a woman from the land of Moab, was born into a pagan society characterized by idol worship. However, her mother-in-law, Naomi, was an Ephrathite devoted to the God of Israel. Despite the contrast in their cultural and religious backgrounds, Ruth's loyalty to Naomi led her to embark on a life-changing journey. Her decision to follow Naomi back to Israel was a bold and courageous step, one that was full of uncertainty and unfamiliarity. Nevertheless, Ruth's loyalty to Naomi ultimately led her to embrace the God of Israel and become a part of His people. This decision may have seemed insignificant at the moment, but it would prove to have a profound impact.

Ruth accompanied Naomi to Bethlehem with only a vague notion of what God was doing there. Upon arriving at the beginning of the barley harvest, they had nothing but their clothes and faith to guide them. Ruth took on the role of provider by gleaning leftover grain from the fields, hoping the harvesters would allow her, as she faced the possibility that someone might reject her and turn her away.

However, one day, Boaz, the field owner, noticed her and kindly encouraged her to work alongside the other women harvesting for him. He had heard of Ruth's devotion to her mother-in-law and was impressed by her decision to embrace the God of Israel. It must have been a joyful moment for Ruth when she realized that despite taking a leap of faith, things were falling into place for her.

Ruth Seeks a Kinsman Redeemer

As time passed, Naomi was troubled that Ruth had no husband to care for her. To address this concern, Naomi devised a plan for Ruth to approach Boaz, who was Naomi's relative and held the vital role of a kinsman redeemer. This role involved marrying the widow of a deceased family member to ensure that the widow would have a son who could carry on the family name and inherit the family's land and possessions. Being a foreigner and lacking male heirs, Ruth found herself in a vulnerable position. If there was no kinsman redeemer to support or protect her, she would have been left without any support or protection, and the family would lose the land and possessions since only a male heir could inherit them. By actively seeking a relative redeemer, Ruth not only fulfilled her duty to her deceased husband's family but also secured her well-being and future.

Boaz willingly took upon himself the great responsibility of redeeming Ruth and her late husband's family line. Boaz's noble actions not only fulfilled Naomi's prayers but also eased Ruth's agony and uncertainty since her husband's death.

The Role of Ruth's Faith in God's Redemption Plan

Ruth's redemption went beyond just finding a husband and a provider. Her faith in the God of Israel played a significant role in God's plan for redemption. Ruth's faith in God led her to eventually become Boaz's wife and the mother of Obed. Thus, Ruth's redemption was not just a personal victory but also an integral part of God's plan for the redemption of humanity.

The union between Ruth and Boaz had far-reaching consequences. Obed, their son, would go on to become the grandfather of King David. And it was through the lineage of David that Jesus Christ, the promised descendant of Abraham, was born. Galatians 3:16 states that God ultimately fulfilled the promises He made to Abraham in Jesus Christ.

Through faith in Jesus Christ, people are saved from their sins and granted eternal life (see Romans 6:23). Ruth's faith in following Naomi and accepting the God of Israel led to her redemption and inclusion in God's plan for redemption. Her story serves as a reminder that God's plan for redemption is not limited to a specific group of people but is open to all who have faith in Him.

Encouragement

"For it is by grace you have been saved, through faith—and this is not from yourselves, it is the gift of God not by works, so that no one can boast." Ephesians 2:8-9

The story of Ruth beautifully illustrates the concepts of redemption and grace. It highlights our universal need for a redeemer to address our deepest needs: forgiveness for our sins and the promise of eternal life. Just as Boaz redeemed Ruth, we also need someone to rescue us from our sins and inspire hope for the future.

Jesus serves as the ultimate redeemer, perfectly fulfilling the role of becoming human to redeem humanity from sin and its consequences. Jesus, as a relative of humanity, willingly embraced the role of redeemer by offering Himself as a sacrifice for the forgiveness of sins. Despite our unworthiness, Jesus paved the way for humanity to reconcile with God and ultimately be redeemed from the grasp of sin and death through His death and resurrection. Therefore, Jesus is the complete manifestation of the Redeemer, offering redemption, renewal, and salvation to all who believe in Him.

Just as Ruth experienced personal redemption and played a role in God's plan, we can also be a part of God's plan for the redemption of those around us. By walking with Him in obedience, we are called to share our faith and guide others to the redemptive power of Christ through faith.

SEE THE STORY IN THE BOOK OF RUTH

12

THE FAITH OF HANNAH

Hannah dreamed of holding her child in her arms. As she watched other women in her community become mothers, her heart ached with longing. Her husband, Elkanah, loved her deeply, but there was no hiding the fact that she could not conceive. To make matters worse, Elkanah had another wife, Peninnah, whom God had blessed with several children. Peninnah would not hesitate to mock and ridicule Hannah, reminding her of her childlessness and making her feel less of a woman. Despite her pain, Hannah rose above her distress and turned to

God in prayer.

The Faith of Hannah

Hannah's faith in God was evident as she prayed in the temple. Her heart was heavy with sorrow and anguish as she yearned for something she knew only God could provide. I can imagine her kneeling with tears streaming down her face, her hands clasped in front of her and her voice choking with emotion as she fervently prayed to God. Hannah poured her soul out to Him with every word, trusting He would hear her plea and grant her request. Her prayer was filled with deep longing and desperation as she prayed to God to have mercy on her and bless her with a son.

Hannah promised that if God granted her a son, she would dedicate him to His service for his entire life. Her faith and devotion to God shone through her prayer as she trusted His goodness and love to answer her heartfelt plea.

Hannah's prayer was so sincere and heartfelt that Eli, the priest, misinterpreted her silent pleas for drunkenness. But she assured him that she was not intoxicated; instead, she was praying earnestly for a child. Hannah's words profoundly impacted Eli, causing him to join her in prayer. He blessed her and said, "Go in peace, and may the God of Israel grant you what you have asked of him" (1 Samuel 1:17). Her demeanor changed after that encounter. She was no longer sad, because she believed God had heard her prayer and would answer it perfectly in His time.

Hannah's Prayer Answered

God rewarded Hannah's faith with the gift of a son. Overcome with joy and gratitude, she named him Samuel, which means "God has heard." Her long-awaited dream had finally come true, and Samuel's arrival was a clear manifestation of the power of prayer and the importance of patiently waiting on God in faith.

True to her word, Hannah fulfilled her vow and dedicated Samuel to God's service. She brought him to the temple and entrusted him to the care of Eli, the high priest. There, Samuel was raised and became a great prophet and priest of Israel. His life was a testament to the power of prayer and the rewards of faith in God.

The Role of Hannah's Faith in God's Redemption Plan

Hannah's son Samuel played a vital role in God's redemptive plan for His people. As a priest, Samuel was responsible for offering sacrifices and interceding on behalf of the people of Israel (see 1 Samuel 7:9). He played a crucial part in leading the nation back to God after a period of disobedience and idolatry.

It was under God's direction that Samuel anointed Saul as the first king of Israel (see 1 Samuel 9), but when Saul failed to obey and prove himself faithful, God instructed Samuel to anoint David as the future king (see 1 Samuel 16). David, a shepherd boy, would become one of the most remarkable kings in Israel's history and an ancestor of Jesus Christ, the promised offspring of Abraham (see Genesis 22:18).

Samuel's faith in God was evident, and he devoted

his life to serving and seeking God's guidance. He was also known for his fervent prayers, and God answered him. Samuel's prayers brought about victories in battle, guidance in decision-making, and the establishment of righteous leadership. His dedication to God's plan for redemption set him apart as a revered figure, and in Psalm 99:6, Samuel is mentioned alongside the esteemed figures of Moses and Aaron, highlighting his significance in Israel's history.

Even though Hannah, Samuel's mother, was barren for many years, God granted her the gift of her son. Her fervent prayers and faith in God had a profound influence even after she passed on. Although Hannah did not live to see her son Samuel's many accomplishments, her legacy of prayer and faith in God led to a chain of events that impacted history.

Encouragement

"The Lord is my strength and my shield; my heart trusts in him, and he helps me." Psalm 28:7

THE FAITH OF HANNAH

Placing our trust in God and seeking Him through prayer can lead to unexpected outcomes. The story of Hannah is a perfect example of this. When God caused her to become barren, it may have been part of a greater purpose unknown to her. Perhaps God wanted Hannah to develop faith in Him, so that she could become a vessel through which He could perform miracles.

As we know, God blessed Hannah with a son, but He also used her faith to birth forth redemption and fulfill His ultimate plans for Israel through her son. We can witness the incredible power of faith and prayer through Hannah's story. God orchestrates some of our challenges to lead us to faith and reliance on Him as our only source of hope and provision. Even in our darkest moments, when we turn to God and look to Him, we surrender control and allow Him to write His story through our lives. As we have seen in Hannah's story, we will not be ashamed when we trust Him.

SEE THE STORY IN 1 SAMUEL 1:2 – 2:21

13

THE FAITH OF ABIGAIL

In 1 Samuel chapter 8, we see a significant turning point in the history of Israel. The Israelites, who had been led by God through various leaders such as Moses, Joshua, priests, and judges, requested Samuel to appoint a king over them. This request came about because the people became concerned about the future leadership of Israel. Samuel's sons were not following in their father's footsteps, and the people wanted to be like other pagan nations that had kings ruling over them. They believed that having a king would bring security and stability to their nation. However, this request was a rejection of God as their true king. The Lord had been their leader up to this point, but the Israelites no longer wanted to be under His rule.

After much prayer and seeking God's guidance, the first king of Israel, Saul, was chosen. Saul appointed David as the leader of his armies, and under David's leadership, they achieved many victories. However, Saul's jealousy and anger towards David grew as he witnessed David's success, leading him to seek David's life. David had to constantly move from one place to another to escape Saul's wrath. One of these places where David sought refuge was the wilderness of Paran, a region located in the northern part of the Sinai Peninsula.

Nabal Angers David

In that region, a man named Nabal lived. He was known for his wealth, but he lacked wisdom. Nabal was married to Abigail, who was known for her beauty and intelligence. Upon learning that Nabal was amid sheep shearing, David sent his men to request provisions. These men made it clear to Nabal that they could steal his livestock but chose not to do so. Instead, they proposed that Nabal provide food for David and his men as an act of gratitude on a feast day.

In ancient Hebrew tradition, sheep shearing was a festive occasion that celebrated the abundance of a shepherd's flock. It was a significant event in the Old Testament, marked by feasting and excessive drinking. Therefore, David's men did not hesitate to request provisions from Nabal. However, Nabal arrogantly refused their request and questioned why he should provide food for strangers when he should be taking care of his servants who were involved in the sheep shearing. This response angered David, who felt disrespected and insulted. He ordered his men to prepare for battle, intending to take revenge on Nabal and his household.

Abigail Prepares to Intercede

One of Nabal's servants approached Abigail in distress and explained the situation to her. The servant recounted how David's men had shown them kindness and protection while tending to Nabal's sheep, and had caused them no harm. In contrast, Nabal had rudely turned away these men and denied them food, which was impolite and placed them in danger. The servant emphasized that Nabal's refusal had not only insulted David and his men but had also brought danger to himself and his entire household.

Realizing the gravity of the situation, Abigail swiftly took action to rectify her husband's foolishness. Without wasting any time, she gathered food and loaded it onto a donkey, instructing her servants to go ahead of her and meet David and his men. Abigail embarked on a journey to confront them, during which she must have rehearsed what to say to David and pondered whether he would show mercy and accept her apology. It was an incredibly risky attempt, considering she was venturing to meet a group of angry, battle-ready men. Nevertheless, Abigail remained determined to intercede for her husband and their entire household.

The Faith of Abigail

As Abigail caught sight of David, she perceived many men accompanying him. With her heart burdened by remorse for her husband's actions, Abigail swiftly dismounted from the donkey. She prostrated herself before David, with her face touching the ground, a sign of utmost humility and submission. Earnestly, Abigail pleaded with David to lend an ear to her words. She beseeched David to forgive her husband's transgressions. As a gesture of reconciliation, Abigail presented David with her offerings.

Abigail's desperate plea for mercy and forgiveness was rooted in her faith in God's divine plan to make David king. Abigail bravely confronted the man determined to harm her household with sincerity and courage. She stood before him with confidence, declaring that the Lord would establish a lasting dynasty and appoint David as the ruler of Israel. Abigail believed in God's intentions for David and showed remarkable discernment as she humbly expressed her faith, even in imminent danger from him. The current king, Saul, still held the power, and David's perceived threat to the throne made her declaration no small matter.

As she begged David to show mercy and kindness, she reminded him that his conscience would be clear from needless bloodshed when God made him king of Israel. David listened attentively to Abigail's heartfelt plea, and I am convinced that he not only heard her sincerity but also acknowledged the faith and wisdom in her words. He thanked God for sending Abigail to prevent him from committing a sinful act and saving him from the guilt of shedding blood. Touched by Abigail's plea, David showed compassion towards her and accepted her apology. He assured her to return home in peace, and she returned with a heart full of gratitude and relief.

The Role of Abigail's Faith in God's Redemption Plan

In a moment of great danger, Abigail found herself surrounded by 400 armed men who threatened her life. She was defenseless, yet, her faith in God's plans and humble nature prevented the outbreak of war. As death loomed near, she silenced its threat through faith and humility, bringing redemption to her household.

Abigail's role in God's plan became evident in the following events. After the deaths of Saul and his son Jonathan in battle, David was anointed as king by the tribe of Judah and eventually by all the tribes of Israel (2 Samuel 5:1-4). Abigail had shown kindness and wisdom towards David, which had not gone unnoticed. God fulfilled her declaration that David would one day become king, solidifying her place in the divine plan.

Her bravery and faith intertwined her life with God's plan of redemption, making her a part of the unfolding story. From the tribe of Judah, David's lineage continued, leading to the birth of Jesus, the ultimate Redeemer. Abigail's story is a powerful example of the impact of faith and humility amid adversity.

Encouragement

"This is love: not that we loved God, but that he loved us and sent his Son as an atoning sacrifice for our sins." 1 John 4:10

Abigail's remarkable bravery and selflessness, as she fearlessly stood up to protect her family in the face of danger, is a powerful reminder of the sacrificial love that Jesus exemplified on the cross. Just as Abigail interceded for her family, Jesus willingly laid down his life for all of us, despite our shortcomings and imperfections, thus establishing Himself as the ultimate mediator, reconciling us with God and atoning for our transgressions (see 1 Timothy 2:5). Through His sacrifice, we are granted the gift of forgiveness, redemption, and a restored relationship with God. This redemption not only offers us personal salvation but also invites us to participate in God's divine plans and purposes in the world.

Just as Abigail interceded for her loved ones, we can do the same through intercessory prayer. We can lift those we care about in prayer, seeking God's transformative and redemptive work in their lives.

Through intercession, we actively participate in God's plan to bring about redemption and renewal in the world (see 1Timothy 2:1-2). Let us draw inspiration from Abigail's faith and courage, knowing that our prayers can have a significant impact on the lives of those we love. With faith, let us approach God, trusting in His ability to bring about redemption and transformation in the lives of those around us and the world.

SEE THE STORY FROM 1 SAMUEL 25

14

THE FAITH OF QUEEN JEZEBEL

Jezebel was a prominent character in Israel's history. She was the daughter of Ethbaal, a priest of a false god Baal. Jezebel played a significant role in shaping Israel's religious affairs during her time. She married Ahab, the king of Israel, and convinced him to abandon the worship of the one true God. She persuaded him to worship Baal, a god commonly associated with fertility and rain which compromised the worship of the Lord in Israel. The worship of Baal was a direct violation of the commandment given by the Lord to His people. God had demanded complete worship and devotion from them, as He is a jealous God (see Exodus 34:14).

The Wrath of God Against Israel

Jezebel's actions disregarded the Lord's commandments and had severe repercussions. The worship of Baal brought morally corrupt practices contrary to the Lord's teachings. They included human sacrifices (see Jeremiah 19:5), immoral sexual practices, and other detestable acts. Israel faced severe consequences as the Lord became angry with them. The Lord's wrath manifested in various ways. One of the ways was through His prophet, Elijah, who was sent to confront Jezebel and Ahab, warning them of the consequences of their actions. This prophet spoke of the impending doom that would befall the land if the rulers did not change their ways and turn back to the Lord.

A severe drought hit the land, which was significant because the people worshiped Baal who was believed to bring rain and fertility to their crops. However, the Lord prevented the rainfall that Baal was supposed to bring, resulting in a long and tough drought. This drought brought about widespread famine and suffering, affecting the people, livestock, and crops.

The Faith of Jezebel

Jezebel harbored a deep-seated hatred for everything associated with the God of Israel. Her disdain was so extreme that she went to great lengths to eradicate any trace of His influence from the land. She actively promoted the worship of this foreign god and commanded the execution of God's prophets, who faithfully served and spoke on behalf of the God she despised. This led to a great divide in the land, where a significant portion of the population turned away from the Lord and embraced Baal worship. Jezebel's actions were driven by her faith in a false god and her insatiable thirst for power and control. Despite numerous warnings and opportunities for repentance, Jezebel refused to acknowledge the truth.

When Elijah, one of God's prophets, challenged the false prophets to call upon Baal to send fire down from Heaven and prove his superiority over the God of Israel, the false prophets failed miserably. However, when Elijah prayed to the Lord, God sent down fire, showcasing His undeniable power (see 1 Kings 18:22-39). Despite witnessing this miraculous display, Jezebel's heart remained hardened. Fueled by anger and fury, she even went so far as to order the pursuit and execution of the prophet Elijah. Her refusal to accept the reality of the one true God led her down a destructive path and further solidified her commitment to her ambitions.

The Absence of Faith

The absence of faith is a foreign concept. Every individual has faith, whether they realize it or not. However, the difference lies in who and where that faith is placed. While some might argue that having faith in something or someone will always result in positive outcomes, the Bible disproves this belief.

Jezebel's story is a prime example of this. Despite

her high status and power, she lacked faith in God, which ultimately led to her tragic downfall. Her husband, Ahab, also lacked faith in God, and his story ended similarly with a fierce battle against the Syrians that resulted in his death.

However, it is essential to acknowledge that there are instances in life where even those who put their trust in God still experience tragic endings that are even worse than Ahab and Jezebel's. However, those who love God and have faith in Him can find peace in the knowledge that everything, even the most complex and painful situations, will ultimately work together for their good (see Romans 8:28).

This assurance extends even to death, where they can rest in the comfort of knowing that they have eternal life with God through faith in Jesus Christ (see John 3:16). In contrast, those who do not believe in God lack the same assurance. Their eternal destinies are not that of peace but of torment in Hell (see Revelation 21:8), where they will experience eternal separation from the source of all love and goodness. This is a sobering reminder to put our faith in God and trust in His goodness, obeying Him only.

In conclusion, faith is a powerful force that can bring about positive outcomes, but we must place it in the right place. The God of Israel is the only one that can truly save, deliver, heal, and bring lasting results. Jezebel and Ahab's tragic stories are a cautionary tale to those who place their faith in anything other than God and His son Jesus Christ.

Encouragement

> *"Blessed is the one who trusts in the Lord, who does not look to the proud, to those who turn aside to false gods." Psalm 40:4*

Despite God revealing Himself as the one true living God, Jezebel's refusal to repent was evident in her behavior. As we read her story, we may feel a sense of superiority in our faith, but we must remember that God is a jealous God who expects complete trust and devotion from His people. God made this expectation clear to the people of Israel, and it remains relevant to us today.

It becomes evident that we have misplaced our faith when we try to replace God with other things. We might prioritize our careers, personal identity, and wealth over God or even resort to sin by going against His commands. This idolatry may not have the same impact as Jezebel's, who led an entire nation astray, but we must remember that God sees through our pretenses. He knows when we prioritize worldly things above Him and when we resort to sin, even if we try to hide it.

Our idolatry does not only affect our relationship with God but also those around us. People observe us to see who is on the throne of our hearts and our profession of faith in God. If we turn away from God and turn to idols, we risk leading those around us astray. This realization should prompt us to repent daily and allow only Jesus to reign on the throne of our hearts and lives. Jesus alone is deserving of our complete trust and devotion. Therefore, let us remember to seek Him with all our hearts and make Him the center of our lives.

SEE THE STORY IN 1 KINGS 16.29-34; 17-22:1-40 2 KINGS 9

15

THE FAITH OF THE WIDOW

During the period of Ahab and Jezebel's rule, the Israelites had turned away from God and started worshiping Baal. As a result, God sent a severe drought to the land as a punishment for their wickedness. The severe famine caused widespread suffering, and people struggled to find enough food to survive. Amid this crisis, God sent Elijah, the prophet, to Zarephath, a city in Sidon. Strangely, God sent Elijah to meet a pagan widow in a Baal-worshiping region to provide him with food and shelter.

THE FAITH OF THE WIDOW

The Widow's Desperation

She may have faithfully prayed and worshiped Baal, hoping for a miracle. Yet, there was no response. The woman grew increasingly desperate as the days turned into weeks and the weeks turned into months. Her food supply decreased, and there was no sign of rain or assistance. Perhaps there were moments when she sacrificed her meals for her son to have enough to eat. Maybe she concealed her tears from him as she prepared their meals, knowing in her heart that a day would come when she would have to watch her son slowly die of starvation. Little did she know that the God of Israel had a special plan for her that would test her faith to the very limit. Despite the widow's circumstances, God had selected her as the instrument of His grace.

As Elijah approached the city gate, he spotted the widow collecting sticks. He approached her and requested a small favor — a drink of water and a piece of bread. Unaware of God's plan, the widow shared her desperate situation with Elijah. She confessed that she had only a handful of flour and a little oil left, which she intended to use to prepare one final meal for herself and her son before they died. Elijah, representing God, spoke to the widow with authority and assured her that if she cooked a small bread cake for him first, her jar of flour and jug of oil would not run dry until the day the Lord sent rain upon the land.

The Faith of the Widow

The task assigned to the widow was nothing short of a daunting challenge. She was already struggling to make ends meet, with barely enough food to sustain herself and her child. If she were to part with her last meal, it could mean death for all three of them. She must have been overwhelmed with numerous questions and uncertainties. Yet, despite all her reservations, the widow, who had no other options for help, made the courageous decision to trust in the prophet's words and complied with his instructions. Miraculously, just as God had promised, the widow's jar of flour and jug of oil never ran out. There was enough daily food to feed Elijah, the widow, and her son. Throughout the entire duration of the drought, God's provision remained steadfast, reaffirming that those who place their trust in Him will never be disappointed.

Imagine the awe and wonder that filled the widow's heart as she baked her daily bread, witnessing an endless supply of flour and oil. Each day, she experienced the fulfillment of God's promise, as He graciously provided for her and her son, sustaining their lives amidst a great famine and hardship. In the face of such miraculous provision, how could she ever abandon this God or go back to worshiping Baal? This divine God, who had no obligation to show her and her son mercy, displayed His abundant grace with each passing day. His transformative power completely changed her life, and her faith in God allowed her to witness the incredible power of His provision.

The Role of the Widow's Faith in God's Redemption Plan

The widow's story is a remarkable example of how God works in the lives of people who have faith in Him, regardless of their background. Despite being an outsider and an enemy of the God of Israel, the widow played an essential role in God's story. Her faith in God's provision and redemption inspires all those in desperate need of God's help and support.

Moreover, the widow's faith became an example for Jesus when he faced rejection from His childhood neighbors in Luke 4:24-25. The people of His hometown did not believe that He was the world's Savior. In response to their disbelief, Jesus pointed out the widow's faith as an illustration. He emphasized that when God's people stubbornly reject faith, God will send His servants to those outside the community.

The widow's story emphasizes the significance of faith and how God can use it to redeem us. Despite her past as an enemy of God and a worshiper of a pagan deity, her faith became a means through which Jesus inspired people to trust Him as the Redeemer and Savior of the world.

Encouragement

THE FAITH OF THE WIDOW

"Jesus said to him, 'If you can believe? All things are possible for one who believes." Mark 9:23.

The widow's story exemplifies the power of faith in God, even in the face of seemingly impossible situations. It serves as a reminder that no matter how difficult our circumstances may appear, we can always count on God's unwavering support and sustenance if we trust Him.

In those moments of uncertainty and doubt, we must cling to our faith and obedience to God's will, even if it goes against societal expectations or conventional wisdom. We should strive to live with faith, knowing that although we may not have a prophet delivering divine instructions to us; God has generously given us His word in the Bible. Within its pages, we will find commands that require faith to follow, and it is through our faith that we position ourselves to witness God's incredible power and mercy.

Like the widow, we too can choose to trust and obey God, even if it means sacrificing everything we hold dear. So, will you take that leap of faith today and play a part in God's extraordinary plans and purposes?

SEE THE STORY IN 1 KINGS 17:7-16

A THREAD OF FAITH

16

THE FAITH OF THE CAPTIVE MAID

The Israelites, known for their devotion to the God of their forefathers, were becoming increasingly involved in sinful actions, turning away from their faith and loyalty. Their kings, who had significant influence over the people, led them astray by introducing false religions and idols. Seeing His people stray far from the path He had set for them, God sent His prophets Elijah and Elisha to guide them back to righteousness and remind them of His faithfulness and love. Despite these efforts, the Israelites remained stubborn and continued to indulge in their sinful and rebellious ways. Eventually, God permitted Syria to defeat His people, using Naaman, the Syrian military commander, as a tool for victory. The punishment was harsh, but its purpose was to serve as a wake-up call for the Israelites, reminding them of the consequences of turning away from God.

The Young Girl Captured

During a brutal Syrian invasion, a village was plunged into chaos by the Syrians. Among the terrified residents was a young girl whose innocence was shattered by the invasion as soldiers stormed through the streets. During the turmoil, the world around her became a blur as she desperately sought a safe hiding place, hoping to escape her captors. However, her attempts failed because a sharp-eyed soldier spotted her trembling form and forcefully dragged her back into the nightmare, seating her on a horse. As a result, her journey to an unfamiliar land, separated from her loved ones, began.

The distance between her and her family grew wider

with each passing moment, leaving her isolated and alone. The once familiar faces of her loved ones were replaced by the cold, unfamiliar faces of her captors. Naaman, the Syrian commander, received the young girl as his slave. Her heart must have ached for her family, for the warmth of their embrace and laughter. Possibly, she clung to the memories of their love, desperately hoping she would be reunited with them one day. But for now, she was left to navigate her new life as an enslaved person.

The Faith of the Captive Maid

One day, Naaman, her master, was struck by a severe illness called leprosy. The news of his affliction quickly spread throughout his household, causing great concern and fear, as leprosy was not only a debilitating illness but also carried a significant social stigma. Despite this the young girl held onto her faith in the God of Israel and the miraculous deeds performed by His prophets. With her master's deteriorating condition, the girl knew she had to act fast. Summoning all her courage, she approached Naaman's wife and suggested that if only her master could meet the prophet in Samaria, God would heal him of his leprosy. The girl's conviction and faith were evident in her words, and her sincerity moved Naaman's wife to take the suggestion seriously. Naaman, desperate for a cure, took the girl's advice and embarked on a journey to meet the prophet in Samaria.

When many in Israel had lost faith and turned away from God and His prophets, this young girl remained in her belief in the God of Israel. Inspired by her faith and courage, Naaman sought healing from the God of Israel, leaving behind his hope in his own god.

Naaman Seeks Healing

As Naaman approached Samaria, he was likely experiencing a great deal of uncertainty and doubt during his journey. Perhaps he couldn't help but question the wisdom of his decision to seek help from a foreign prophet who served a foreign God, especially since Naaman was a proud and powerful commander who used to get what he wanted. However, he couldn't shake off the message of hope that the young Israelite girl had shared with him.

Upon arrival, a messenger greeted Naaman when he arrived at Elisha's doorstep and delivered a simple instruction from the prophet: "Go, wash seven times in the Jordan, and your flesh will be restored, and you will be cleansed" (2 Kings 5:10-12). Naaman was initially furious and offended by the prophet's command. The messenger had asked him to wash himself in a dirty river instead of performing a grand gesture or ritual. However, Naaman's servants convinced him to follow the prophet's instructions, and he eventually humbled himself and went to the Jordan River.

As Naaman dipped himself into the cool and refreshing waters of the Jordan River, one can only imagine the sensation he felt as he could sense God's healing power coursing through him, washing away the disease that had plagued him for so long. He submerged himself into the river seven times as instructed by the prophet Elisha. To his amazement, his leprosy vanished entirely, and God restored his skin to its former glory. Filled with an overwhelming sense of joy, Naaman declared that there was no God in the world except in Israel and offered generous gifts to Elisha as a token of his gratitude for this miraculous healing.

The Role of the Captive Maid's Faith in God's Redemption Plan

Naaman left Samaria a changed man, with a newfound respect for the God of Israel and a renewed hope for the future. Despite her difficult circumstances, the young girl's faith played an essential role in Naaman's faith in God. Although she was a captive, she remained faithful to God and was sensitive to the needs of those around her. Her faith became a powerful tool God used to bring about salvation for a man once an enemy of God. Naaman's redemption was not just physical, but spiritual as well. He acknowledged the God of Israel as the one true God and vowed to worship Him alone.

Furthermore, Naaman's faith served as a significant example for Jesus when he encountered rejection from the people in His hometown during His ministry (see Luke 4:24-27). The individuals in His childhood community doubted that He was the Savior of the world and the fulfillment of the prophecy in Isaiah 61:1-2. In response to their disbelief, Jesus used Naaman's faith as a powerful illustration. He emphasized that when God's people stubbornly reject faith, God will send His servants to those outside the community.

However, Naaman's faith in God would not have been possible without the influence of the young girl who shared her faith in God, extending far beyond what anyone could have anticipated.

Encouragement

"For I am not ashamed of the gospel because it is the power of God that brings salvation to everyone who believes." Romans 1:16

The young girl's story is inspiring and serves as a

testament to the strength of faith in the face of adversity. As devoted followers of Jesus Christ, we may encounter trials and tribulations that leave us hopeless. These challenges could take many forms, such as illness, grief, sorrow, or despair. However, in these moments, we can still find hope and purpose in our faith.

When we choose to look beyond our suffering and focus on the needs of those around us, we become more sensitive to the brokenness and pain that others may be experiencing. Despite our struggles, our faith still has the power to bring hope and freedom to those around us. Just as the young girl's captivity did not hold her back from sharing her faith, our trials and suffering cannot dim the light our faith can bring in the darkness.

By being sensitive to the needs of those around us, we can become the hands and feet of Jesus, bringing the news of redemption and hope to those bound in sin and in desperate need of the saving knowledge of Jesus Christ. The ultimate sacrifice that Jesus made on the cross has freed us from the bondage of sin, and through our faith in Him, we can experience true freedom, inner peace, and the assurance of eternal life (see 1 John 5:11-13). No matter what trials or tribulations we may face, we can still share this truth with those who need to hear it and be a source of hope, encouragement, and inspiration to others.

SEE THE STORY IN 2 KINGS 5:1-25

17

THE FAITH OF QUEEN ATHALIAH

Athaliah, the daughter of Ahab and Jezebel, was infamous for her devotion to idol worship and her persecution of the Israelites. Her parents' legacy of idolatry and cruelty did not die with them, as Athaliah continued to follow in their footsteps. She nurtured a deep-seated hatred towards the God of Israel and made every effort to maintain the worship of false gods. One of her most wicked acts was establishing altars for the god Baal in Jerusalem.

Her influence and power extended to her son, the

king of Judah. She encouraged him to commit wicked acts, just as her mother had done to her husband years earlier. Athaliah's love for authority and control only grew stronger as she ruled through her son, ensuring that he remained under her guidance and did not stray from her wishes. She relentlessly pursued power and disregarded the well-being of her subjects throughout her reign.

The Reign of Queen Athaliah

During the reign of Queen Athaliah, the people of Israel suffered greatly. She was a passionate worshiper of the god Baal and did not tolerate disagreement or opposition to her authority. Possibly, those who remained loyal to the God of Israel and refused to worship Baal were mercilessly persecuted and killed.

Athaliah's thirst for power knew no bounds. She went to unimaginable lengths to secure her position on the throne, even resorting to the unthinkable act of murdering her grandsons. By eliminating any potential heirs to the throne, she believed she could solidify her rule and ensure that no one would challenge her authority. Athaliah reigned over Judah for six years, making her the only woman ever to rule Judah. The people of Israel lived in fear and uncertainty during her reign, as she ruled with an iron fist and showed no mercy to those who opposed her.

The Downfall of Queen Athaliah

The false religion forced the people of Judah to abandon their faith in the God of their forefathers. However, Athaliah's reign of terror would not last forever. Some of the Israelites, who were weary of her oppressive rule and longing for a return to the worship of the true God, rose against her. Led by the high priest Jehoiada, they overthrew Athaliah and put her to death, bringing an end to her tyrannical reign. After the downfall of his grandmother Athaliah, Joash ascended to the throne. His aunt Jehosheba had protected him during the massacre of his brothers in the temple before his ascension. With the true faith of the Israelites restored, Joash began a period of religious revival and restoration. The people tore down the altars and temples dedicated to Baal and restored the worship of the true God.

The Faith of Queen Athaliah

Athaliah was driven by a deep-seated need for control. Her actions, which exposed many flaws in her character, were ultimately rooted in a fundamental lack of faith in God. Despite claiming to worship Baal as her god, it was evident that she was in control of her own life and even that of her son, King Ahaziah. Control of her life made her essentially her own god.

Athaliah was like her mother, Jezebel, who held power by undermining God's authority and that of her husband. If only Athaliah had trusted the God of Israel and dedicated herself to pleasing Him, she would have found a trustworthy source of authority over all things (see Matthew 28:18).

By putting her faith in an idol and herself, she missed out on the opportunity to experience the love and guidance of God. This behavior ultimately trapped her in a cycle of sin and destruction, leading to her untimely death.

Encouragement

"Show me the way I should go, for to you I entrust my life." Psalm 143:8

As Christians, it is important to reflect on what sets us apart from those who do not believe in God. Our faith is not only about our beliefs but also our behavior and lifestyle. To have true faith in God, we must surrender control and submit our will to Him (see Matthew 7:21). This means allowing Him to lead our passions and pursuits, by His guidance and commands.

We are all susceptible to sin, and even the most virtuous among us are not exempt from it. Sometimes, we may even persist in our sinful behavior, much like Athaliah, and during these times, it may appear as though we do not have faith.

However, it's important to recognize that everyone has faith in something or someone, whether it be God, the government, or societal norms. The crucial factor is being aware of what we choose to have faith in.

Jesus taught that if we aspire to be His disciples, we must abandon our old ways and follow Him wholeheartedly (see Matthew 16:24). This means that we cannot have one foot in the world and one foot in the Kingdom of God. We must choose one way or the other. To ensure that we are on the right path, we must study and understand the teachings of the Bible. It is only through Scriptural knowledge that we can learn how to live as true followers of Jesus Christ. We must also be intentional about seeking God's will in everything that we do, whether it is how we dress, live, speak, or treat others. Our faith in God and our willingness to follow His commands set us apart from the rest of the world. We cannot claim to have a close relationship with God if we refuse to comply with His principles and instructions.

Amos 3:3 poses a thought-provoking question: "Do

two walk together unless they have agreed to do so?" This question emphasizes the importance of being in harmony with God's will if we want to walk alongside Him. Therefore, we must commit ourselves wholeheartedly to God and follow His teachings throughout our lives. Only then can we genuinely consider ourselves to be His followers and lead a life that is pleasing to Him.

SEE THE STORY IN 2 KINGS 11; 2 CHRONICLES 22

18

THE FAITH OF JEHOSHEBA

Jehosheba, the stepdaughter of Athaliah, demonstrated an extraordinary act of selflessness by rescuing her nephew, Joash, from her power-hungry stepmother. Knowing that Athaliah had already killed her grandsons to secure her position as ruler of Judah, Jehosheba fearlessly took it upon herself to protect her nephew Joash and keep him safe. She witnessed the suffering and oppression caused by Athaliah's rule in the kingdom of Judah, including the desecration of the temple and the disrespect towards God. However, Jehosheba remained determined in her commitment to protect Joash.

Filled with fear, Jehosheba carefully picked up the baby, hoping to go unnoticed; she hid the child in a bedroom. I envision her trembling in terror as Joash's siblings fell victim to their grandmother's massacre — perhaps silently praying to God for the baby to stay quiet and not attract attention.

Eventually, when it was time for her to leave the castle, she summoned her last bit of courage and quietly left the castle with her nephew. I imagine her heart raced as she clutched the baby close to her chest, with her every step filled with fear. The weight of her decision to save Joash from certain death at the hands of his power-hungry grandmother bore down on her shoulders like a heavy burden. She knew the risks involved in defying the queen's orders, but her love for the child and her knowledge of his destiny as the rightful heir to the throne compelled her to act.

As she navigated the dark corridors of the castle, Jehosheba's mind must have raced with thoughts of the dangers ahead. She knew that Athaliah's spies were everywhere and that any misstep could lead to her death. Yet, she also knew that she could not stand idly by and watch as the kingdom of Judah crumbled under the rule of her evil stepmother.

The Faith of Jehosheba

A daunting task now lay ahead of Jehosheba, the wife of Jehoiada the priest — to protect an infant destined to become the king of Judah. Fearful of the threat that could potentially harm the child, Jehosheba took the baby to the safest place she knew, the house of the Lord. For six long years, she possibly lived in constant worry, hoping that her faith in God's protection would be enough to keep the child safe until he could rightfully claim his position as king. During this time, Jehosheba's faith in God must have kept her going. She possibly spent countless hours in prayer, seeking guidance and protection for the child in her care. One can only imagine how her faith in God grew stronger as she watched Joash thrive under her watchful eye.

The Role of Jehosheba's Faith in God's Plan of

Redemption

The Israelite priest, Jehoiada coronated Joash at the tender age of seven, marking the beginning of a significant chapter in Israel's history. During Joash's reign, he initiated the eradication of Baal worship. The people purged the nation of idolatrous practices and restored the temple of God to its former glory. The people of Israel were once again encouraged to follow God's commandments, and the nation experienced a period of peace and prosperity. Jehosheba's faith in God and resistance to Queen Athaliah's sinister plans were crucial in leading those who had strayed from their faith and followed Baal back to God. Her loyalty led to a chain of events that reignited the people's faithfulness to God, sparking a revival among them.

Jehosheba's brave actions not only saved the lineage of King David but also secured the arrival of the promised offspring of Abraham. Her faith in the one true God and determination to do what was right in His eyes ensured that the lineage of Jesus Christ was preserved and protected.

Encouragement

> *"Be on your guard; stand firm in the faith; be courageous; be strong."* 1 Corinthians 16:13

The story of Jehosheba is a testament to the incredible power of faith in God. Her trust and devotion to God allowed her to rescue Joash, and pave the way for the revival of God's reign in the kingdom. By doing so, she also ensured the continuation of King David's lineage, which was crucial to God's plan for His people.

Jehosheba's bravery and faith in the face of danger and uncertainty serve as a source of inspiration for believers to this day. Her story reminds us that, even when we are faced with seemingly insurmountable obstacles, we can trust in God to guide us and provide us with the strength and courage we need to overcome them. Moreover, Jehosheba's legacy highlights the transformative power of faith and the importance of staying true to our beliefs. She was willing to risk everything to obey God's will, knowing that He was working behind the scenes to bring about His perfect plans and purposes. Her story encourages us to do the same, trusting that God is in control and that He will use our obedience to bring about His good and perfect will in our lives.

Just like Jehosheba, embracing faith in God can be a challenging journey that requires us to confront unholy customs and societal expectations. It can sometimes mean taking risks and challenging ungodly family practices and attitudes. However, as we stand firm in faith, we become vessels through which God can unveil His divine intentions. Our lives become like pens that inscribe His remarkable narrative, and we become crucial players in God's plan of redemption for the world.

So, if you are ready to embrace faith in God today, know that you are not alone. God is with you every step of the way, and He will guide you through whatever challenges that may come your way.

SEE THE STORY IN 2 KINGS 11:1-3; 2 CHRONICLES 22:1–23:15

A THREAD OF FAITH

19

THE FAITH OF QUEEN ESTHER

King Ahasuerus was known for his luxurious tastes and extravagant celebrations in ancient Persia. He threw a grand feast and invited his nobles and subjects from across the kingdom to showcase his wealth and power. As part of the festivities, the king ordered his wife, Queen Vashti, to attend and display her beauty to the public. However, Queen Vashti refused to comply with the king's orders, a move that greatly angered the Persian monarch.

The king stripped Vashti of her position for her

disobedience, despite her status as the queen and his beloved wife. The king was worried that her insubordination might influence other women in the kingdom to challenge the authority of their husbands. Therefore, he sought a new queen who would be more obedient and submissive to his will.

To prevent any further conflict, King Ahasuerus issued a decree throughout the kingdom that required all women, regardless of their social standing, to honor and respect their husbands. This decree ensured that women remained submissive to their husbands and did not question their authority.

The Persian King's Search for a New Queen

In search of the new queen, the king eventually found Esther, a young Hebrew girl belonging to the tribe of Benjamin. Historical events such as the Babylonian invasion of Jerusalem and the Persians taking over Babylon caused Esther and her fellow Hebrews to be exiled to Persia. They were part of a Jewish community that had to leave their homeland and live in Babylon until the Persians took over.

Esther's charisma and beauty caught the king's attention, and she won his favor. This attraction to Esther led the king to choose her as his new queen, to replace Vashti. However, despite being the queen, Esther kept her true identity as a Jew hidden from everyone around her. She followed the guidance of her cousin Mordecai, who had raised her and decided to conceal her identity. Esther's cousin had always been her guide and mentor, and Esther trusted him completely. Therefore, she followed his instructions as she had always done while under his care.

Haman's Plot to Exterminate the Jews

One day, when the king's servant Haman demanded that all the people bow down to him, Mordecai refused because of his faith in the God of Israel. This disobedience angered Haman and revealed Mordecai's true identity to him. Haman then devised a sinister plan to rid the kingdom of all Jews, and he approached the king to request a decree for their destruction.

The news that Haman intended to kill all the Jews reached Esther. Upon hearing this, she, a Jew herself, was overwhelmed with fear and felt the weight of the news tighten its grip on her heart. I can imagine the immense walls of the palace suddenly feeling as though they were crumbling down upon her, enclosing her in a suffocating embrace. In the face of such danger, she must have pondered her next move, fully aware that her own life and the lives of her people hung in the balance.

Mordecai discovered Haman's plan and sent an urgent letter to his cousin, fearing for their safety and imploring her to take action. He urged her to use her position as queen to approach the king and plead with him to intervene and save her people from certain destruction. However, Esther was well aware of the risks and dangers that were involved in Mordecai's plan to save the Jews. She knew approaching the king without being summoned was a serious offense that could lead to her execution unless the king extended his golden scepter as a sign of mercy.

To explain her concerns, Esther wrote back to her

cousin Mordecai, expressing her hesitations and reservations about the plan. She reminded him of the severity of the situation and the potential consequences that could follow if things didn't go according to plan.

In response, her cousin reminded her that, as a Jew herself, she was also in grave danger and that her position as the queen may have been part of God's providential plan to save her people. With this encouragement from her cousin, Esther summoned all her courage and began to prepare herself for the risky task ahead. She knew that the fate of her people rested on her shoulders, and she was determined to do everything in her power to save them.

The Faith of Esther

Esther was reminded of her purpose and found renewed faith in her heart. She urged all Jews to fast for three days and nights, seeking God's guidance and wisdom during this time. Despite the potential risk to her own life, Esther remained in her belief that God's plan would come to fruition. Her words, "If I perish, I perish" (Esther 4:16), reflected her acceptance of God's will and her willingness to face any outcome, even death, to fulfill God's plan for His people.

After fasting, Esther made preparations, unsure if she was preparing for death or victory. Nevertheless, she held onto her faith in God, knowing that, she had sought His guidance and trusted that whatever the outcome, it would bring glory to Him. As Esther woke up that day, I imagine she was uncertain. Perhaps she wondered if it would be the last time she would witness the sunrise, feel the gentle breeze against her skin, or hear the steady rhythm of her heartbeat. Doubt may have crept in at times, but her confidence in God remained strong. She knew that God was by her side because she had surrendered herself to do what was right in His eyes.

The Role of Esther's Faith in God's Redemption Plan

Esther stood amid the king's inner court, adorned in her majestic robe. Possibly, her heart raced so intensely that it felt like it might leap out of her chest. She gazed upon the king, who sat regally upon his throne, positioned directly across from the palace entrance, and a sense of uncertainty washed over her. She knew the risks she was taking by appearing uninvited before the king, but she knew it was the only way to save her people.

At that moment, the king's eyes met Esther's, and she found favor in his sight. He held out the golden scepter, a symbol of his authority. He asked, "What is your request? It shall be given to you, even to the half of my kingdom" (Esther 5:3). Esther knew this was the moment she had been waiting for. However, instead of immediately disclosing her request to the king, she meticulously planned a feast and invited the king and his servant, Haman. It was during this event that Esther found the courage to speak up. She sincerely pleaded with the king to spare her and her people, while also revealing Haman's malicious scheme to destroy the Jewish community.

Ultimately, the king granted Esther's plea, ensuring the safety of her people.

Esther's faith in God was not just a tiny part of this

story — it played a vital role in God's plan to save His chosen people. Esther's actions preserved Abraham's lineage and ensured the fulfillment of God's promise of a blessed offspring. As mentioned in Galatians 3:16, Jesus is the ultimate fulfillment of this promise. By saving the Jews from destruction, God ensured that Abraham's descendants would continue, eventually leading to the birth of Jesus Christ.

Encouragement

> *"But my righteous one will live by faith. And I take no pleasure in the one who shrinks back." Hebrews 10:38*

Esther's life as queen was filled with luxury and privilege, but her true calling extended far beyond the splendor of the royal court. God had placed her in that position not for the sake of royal attire and the title of Queen, but for a purpose that held profound significance.

In the same way, as Christians, our purpose is more significant than enjoying the blessings and companionship of walking with Jesus Christ. Our role as a royal priesthood is not one of ease, but self-sacrifice. Jesus emphasized that anyone who comes to Him and does not prioritize Him above their family and even their own life cannot be His disciple (see Luke 14:26-33). Following Jesus requires us to place Him above everything else, even our lives. Suppose we only follow Jesus for comfort or the mere title of Christian. In that case, we will falter or deny Him when confronted with challenging circumstances that demand faith, sacrifice, or even risking our lives to fulfill His will.

Just like Esther, who had to take a stand in faith and risk her life to carry out God's plan to save His people from Haman's threats, we are to risk everything for God's plans to manifest through our lives. The risk includes making known the redemptive work of Jesus to those who do not yet know Him.

SEE THE STORY IN THE BOOK OF ESTHER

20

THE FAITH OF ELISABETH

Elisabeth and Zechariah were a couple who dedicated their lives to following God's commandments and serving others. Despite their faith, Elisabeth faced the heartbreaking reality of being unable to conceive, and her childbearing years had long passed. Nevertheless, Elisabeth remained faithful to God and possibly prayed for His blessings and mercy to grant her the gift of a child. Each passing month only seemed to magnify the sense of emptiness in her womb, yet Elisabeth refused to give up on her devotion to God.

THE FAITH OF ELISABETH

A Heavenly Messenger Appears to Zechariah

One day, Zechariah, a dutiful priest, was carrying out his duties when an angel of the Lord appeared before him, surrounding him in fear. However, the angel comforted him, assuring him not to be afraid. With bated breath and a racing heart, Zechariah was about to receive the long-awaited answer to his prayers.

The angel revealed to him that his wife, Elisabeth, would miraculously become pregnant and give birth to a son. The child was to be named John, and the angel described to Zechariah all the fantastic things that John would become and how God intended to use him. At that moment, I imagine the angel's words transported him into a dream-like state, and he hung onto every word spoken. Every detail filled his heart with excitement and anticipation, and he could hardly contain his joy.

However, a sudden realization brought him back to reality. He remembered his old age and his wife's inability to conceive, which filled his mind with curiosity, and doubt. With a courageous heart, Zechariah asked the angel, "How can I be sure of this? I am old, and my wife is advanced in years" (Luke 1:18). Despite his doubts, the angel of the Lord continued to reassure Zechariah, but due to his lack of faith, the angel made him unable to speak. The angel revealed to him that he would remain mute until the things he had spoken of came to pass.

A Promise Fulfilled

In the months that followed, as Elisabeth's stomach grew, I imagine Zechariah must have longed to tell Elisabeth that God's promise, delivered by the angel, was being fulfilled. Yet, no matter how hard he tried, he couldn't speak. Therefore, he could only marvel and witness God's steadfast faithfulness as his aged wife carried their much-awaited son.

After months of anticipation, Elisabeth's day finally arrived to give birth. As she went through labor pains, I imagine that Elisabeth was filled with a sense of anticipation and excitement, knowing that she was about to give birth to a child she had yearned for, for many years. Despite the pain and discomfort, Elisabeth remained strong and focused on the momentous occasion. After what felt like an eternity, the moment finally arrived. As promised by the angel, Elisabeth gave birth to a son and she named him John.

As soon as the baby was born, Zechariah, who had been unable to speak for nine months, started to praise God for the baby's arrival and name. He felt a sense of wonder and amazement as he witnessed the incredible things that God had accomplished, and he began to bless God for His unending goodness and mercy. The neighbors gathered around to witness the birth and were amazed at the beautiful things that had happened. They stood in awe of the power of God and the incredible miracle that had taken place before their eyes. The arrival of baby John had brought joy and wonder to everyone who knew Elisabeth and Zechariah.

The Faith of Elisabeth

Elisabeth was an exceptional woman who lived with

faith and a deep submission to God. Despite struggling with years of infertility, she never lost her commitment to leading a righteous life in God's presence. Her faith in God was firm, and she recognized His supreme authority, which she believed deserved her devotion and reverence.

Elisabeth's faith must have given her the strength to persevere through difficult times and to maintain hope for a brighter future. Although her faith in God may have seemed insignificant at the time, her commitment paved the way for her to play an essential role in God's redemption plan. Through her submission and devotion to God, Elisabeth had no idea that God would one day choose her to be the mother of a child who would prepare people's hearts to receive God's redemption through faith in Jesus Christ.

The Role of Elisabeth's Faith in God's Redemption Plan

John also known as John the Baptist prepared the way for Jesus Christ, who fulfilled the prophecy of being the offspring of Abraham. John's mission was to pave the way for the fulfillment of this prophecy by preaching a message of repentance and baptism and pointing people toward the coming of Jesus Christ as the long-awaited Messiah. By doing so, John helped to prepare the hearts and minds of the people for the arrival of the one who would ultimately bring the blessing of salvation to all the world's nations, fulfilling the promise that God had made to Abraham so many years before.

John's message of repentance and the need to turn away from sin was central to his teachings. He was a voice crying out in the wilderness, as described in Mark 1:1-9. He baptized people with water, symbolizing their repentance and cleansing from sin. He prepared people to obtain salvation, forgiveness for their sins, and the gift of eternal life by placing their faith in Jesus Christ.

Encouragement

"Anyone who believes in him will never be put to shame." Romans 10:11

Living a life of righteousness and faithfully following God's commands is essential to our spiritual journey. However, it is important to note that this doesn't mean our prayers and desires will always be fulfilled by God as we envision them. We cannot control every aspect of our lives, but we can control our response to the challenges that come our way.

Choosing to obey God wholeheartedly by living righteously before Him and having faith in Him empowers us to trust God's perfect timing to fulfill our needs. Trusting in God's unwavering faithfulness gives us the strength to face any obstacle that comes our way, knowing that God is in control and anything He withholds or allows in our lives is for our good because He is good.

Elisabeth's life is an excellent example of the power of living a life of righteousness and trusting in God's faithfulness. She found comfort in God's sovereignty, and her faith enabled her to endure the pain of bareness. Today, we can draw inspiration from her example by trusting God's timing and plan for our lives.

By living righteously before God and having faith, we position ourselves to be available for God to use us according to His plans, in His own time, and in His way. This way, we become vessels through which God can work to fulfill His purpose in our lives and those around us.

SEE THE STORY IN LUKE 1:5-24; : 57- 80

21

THE FAITH OF MARY

Mary, a young woman from Nazareth, was betrothed to Joseph, a descendant of David and a member of the tribe of Judah. They were both eagerly anticipating their upcoming wedding and the prospect of beginning a family together. However, their plans unexpectedly turned when an angel appeared to Mary. The angel conveyed the astounding news that God had chosen Mary to conceive a son, who was to be named Jesus, meaning "God saves." This revelation must have been incredibly overwhelming for Mary, as she was

THE FAITH OF MARY

unmarried and had never been intimate with a man. The angel revealed that Jesus would be an extraordinary child, the Son of God, and the long-awaited Savior who would redeem His people from their sins. He would be great and called the Son of the Most High. The Lord God would bestow upon Him the throne of His ancestor David, and He would rule over Israel for eternity, with His kingdom having no end.

I imagine Mary stood frozen in awe, her eyes wide with wonder as she gazed at the angelic figure before her. In that extraordinary moment, Mary summoned all the courage she could muster and bravely asked the angel how it could be possible for her, a virgin, to conceive a child. The angel responded with a gentle assurance, explaining that the Holy Spirit would come upon her and overshadow her, leading to her miraculous pregnancy. To further reassure Mary, the angel shared the incredible news of her cousin Elizabeth's own miraculous pregnancy despite her advanced age and previous inability to conceive. The angel's words served as a profound affirmation that, with God, all things are possible.

The Faith of Mary

Mary likely experienced a whirlwind of emotions. She understood that accepting this message would ultimately change her life forever. Since she was not yet married to Joseph, her pregnancy would be considered illegitimate in her community. Her illegitimate pregnancy meant that she would face severe consequences, including damage to her reputation and even the risk of losing her life. During those times, an engagement was equivalent to being married, and they punished any act of adultery with stoning. However, despite the potential challenges she would face and the risk of losing her life and her newfound love, Mary placed her trust in God's plan and embraced her role as the mother of Jesus, the Savior of the world. With faith, she declared, "I am the Lord's servant. May your word to me be fulfilled" (Luke 1:38). Little did she know that a surprising turn of events was approaching.

In a dream, an angel appeared to Joseph and reassured him that he could marry Mary. The divine messenger explained that Mary had conceived through the Holy Spirit and carried Jesus, the Son of God. God rewarded Mary's obedience in a way she could never have imagined — she was allowed to become Joseph's wife, despite the possibility of losing him and her life.

I imagine Mary's anticipation and excitement increased with every passing moment in the days that followed. She eagerly awaited the visible growth of her belly, which would physically manifest the child she had received with gladness through faith. As time passed, her excitement and enthusiasm must have grown even more as she eagerly anticipated that she would finally see Jesus, the long-awaited promise of redemption to humanity. Mary's heart likely swelled with joy and wonder at the thought of the miraculous child growing within her and the incredible mission He would one day, fulfill.

Mary Visits Elisabeth

In those beautiful days, Mary visited Elisabeth, and they spent quality time together. As they conversed, I imagine the Holy Spirit's presence filling the room, creating a tangible sense of awe and wonder. Then, something extraordinary happened; Elisabeth's baby, later known as John the Baptist, jumped for joy upon hearing Mary's voice. It was as if he recognized the presence of the Messiah growing inside Mary's womb, even before His birth. The Holy Spirit moved Elisabeth to bless and affirm Mary. She acknowledged Mary's faith and obedience in accepting God's plan for her life.

Mary was overwhelmed with an intense feeling of joy that took over her. Unable to contain her emotions, she felt compelled to express her appreciation and thank God. Her heart was ablaze with gratitude, and Mary couldn't help but burst forth in praise, proclaiming God's mercy and faithfulness. She understood the immense privilege and honor of being the mother of the world's Savior. Her heart overflowed with love and devotion to God as she embraced her role in His redemptive plan for humanity.

Mary and Elisabeth's encounter showcased God's faithfulness and ability to perform miracles. Their shared experience must have deepened their bond and strengthened their will to have faith in God's plans, regardless of the circumstances.

The Role of Mary's Faith in God's Redemption Plan

The birth of Jesus marked the fulfillment of the long-awaited promise that God had given to Abraham and the arrival of the world's Savior. One can only imagine the charged atmosphere filled with anticipation and excitement as this momentous event unfolded. God blessed Mary and her husband with the incredible privilege of witnessing the arrival of this blessing to all nations firsthand. Mary, through her faith, carried Jesus in her womb for nine months, playing an essential role in bringing the long-awaited Messiah and offspring of Abraham into the world. It is through the same faith in Jesus we get to obtain forgiveness for our sins and the blessing of eternal life.

Just as Mary's faith allowed her to bear Jesus in her womb, believers can now carry Jesus in their hearts and experience His transformative work in their lives through faith. The destructive force of sin entered the world due to Eve's distrust and disobedience, but Mary's obedience and faith ushered in redemption for humanity.

Encouragement

"And without faith it is impossible to please God, because anyone who comes to him must believe that he exists and that he rewards those who earnestly

seek him." Hebrews 11:6

Mary had her life planned out, but when she received a divine call from God to play a crucial role in His plan for redemption, she embraced it with faith. Mary deeply grasped the significance of following God's divine plan, willingly setting aside her own aspirations and her life. Her submission stemmed from her profound understanding that she was a servant of God, and thus, she was called to carry out His will rather than her own.

When we accept Jesus Christ as the ultimate authority in our lives, there is a significant shift in our wills. It's not a power struggle or a contest of wills, wherein God has to forcefully compel us to obey Him. Instead, it's a voluntary surrender of our will to His. Much like Mary, who promptly trusted and obeyed, we are called by God to obediently follow His commands and His purpose for our lives. Through our trust and obedience to God, we actively demonstrate that our allegiance lies with

Him and not with the values of the world, or even our desires. This act of surrendering our will to God is a powerful testament to our faith and devotion to Him.

Just as Mary's faith and obedience allowed her to bear Jesus in her womb and be a vessel through which God brought forth His redemption. As believers, we are called to do the same, to carry Jesus in our hearts and be willing to sacrifice our lives and desires so that the life of Jesus can find full expression in our lives. This will enable us to demonstrate to those around us God's redemptive power through faith in Jesus and His plan to redeem humanity.

Have you ever stopped to think if you are living your life under God's will or your own? It is essential to take some time to reflect on your actions and decisions and assess if they align with the teachings and values of the Bible. It is important to consider how your life reflects your commitment to

THE FAITH OF MARY

Jesus and whether there are areas you can improve upon to demonstrate your faith in God.

And shall I pray Thee change Thy will, my Father,
Until it be according unto mine?
But, no, Lord, no, that never shall be, rather
I pray Thee blend my human will with Thine.

I pray Thee hush the hurrying, eager longing,
I pray Thee soothe the pangs of keen desire—
See in my quiet places, wishes thronging—
Forbid them, Lord, purge, though it be with fire."
— Amy Carmichael

SEE THE STORY IN LUKE 1:26-56

22

THE FAITH OF ANNA

Anna was a woman belonging to the tribe of Asher, which was one of the twelve tribes of Israel. She had a married life with her husband until tragedy struck, and her husband passed away after only seven years of their marriage. One never imagines becoming a widow so soon after getting married. We all envision growing old, embracing our husbands, and caring for many grandchildren. However, for Anna, this nightmare became a harsh reality. Despite the heart-wrenching circumstances, she had no choice but to accept and adapt to her new life as a widow. Anna must have endured unbearable pain, and the experience likely left her with countless unanswered questions. But instead of giving in to despair and hopelessness, she chose a different path. She sought comfort in prayer and fasting and devoted herself wholeheartedly to God, never leaving the temple.

The Faith of Anna

Anna's faith in God led her to spend her days in His presence, dedicating herself to His service. She firmly believed in the promise of the coming Messiah and held onto this faith for many years. It is likely that, from a young age, she had been exposed to the prophecies of the Messiah by other believers. Therefore, she eagerly anticipated the arrival of the Messiah and possibly prayed for His coming. Perhaps she dedicated hours to studying the scriptures, searching for clues and signs indicating His imminent arrival. Her heart overflowed with anticipation, as she believed the Messiah would end suffering and pain and deliver humanity from their sins. Despite her aging body growing weak, her faith in the promised Messiah only strengthened with time

Anna's Encounter with Jesus

One day, Mary and Joseph took baby Jesus to the Temple in Jerusalem forty days after His birth to fulfill Mary's ritual purification after childbirth and to present Jesus as their firstborn before God (see Leviticus 12 and Exodus 13:12-15). As they entered the temple gates, Anna, an elderly prophetess who had spent many years serving in the temple, locked eyes with baby Jesus. At that moment, a deep sense of understanding filled her heart and overwhelmed her with awe. She knew she had encountered the world's Savior. Unable to contain her emotions, Anna burst forth in praise and thanksgiving to God. I can only imagine that, as she lifted her hands towards the heavens, her soul overflowed with adoration for the Almighty. Her words echoed through the temple, captivating the attention of those nearby. Remarkably, even without being informed by Mary or Joseph about the child's identity, Anna instinctively recognized that the Redeemer, Jesus Christ, had been born. This recognition was likely due to to her gift of prophecy, a divine insight granted to her by God. Unable to contain the good news, Anna went on to tell everyone who had been waiting for the redemption of Jerusalem about the arrival of the long-awaited offspring of Abraham.

The Role of Anna's Faith in God's Redemption Plan

Anna had lived a long and eventful life, filled with joy and hardship. It wasn't until she reached the remarkable age of 84 that she experienced a profound encounter with Jesus Christ, the Redeemer. Throughout the years, she likely endured many trials, but her faith sustained her. She believed in the promise of the Messiah, as foretold by God's prophets, which must have given her hope during times of struggle.

When Anna's long-awaited encounter with Jesus finally occurred, it sparked a newfound sense of purpose within her. Her faith inspired her to participate in God's plan of redemption actively. She eagerly shared the good news of the Redeemer's arrival, believing that through faith in Jesus Christ, people could receive forgiveness for their sins, be granted the gift of eternal life, and establish a deep and meaningful relationship with God. This encounter with Jesus ignited a fire within Anna to spread the message of hope and redemption to all who would listen.

Encouragement

"In him our hearts rejoice, for we trust in his holy name." Psalm 33:21

Anna's life exemplified the profound impact of faith in God, illustrating how it can sustain us through the most trying times. Just like Anna, all of us encounter loss, pain, and hardship. However, when we consciously embrace faith in God, we open ourselves to experiencing firsthand the remarkable power of redemption through our belief in Jesus Christ. This faith not only grants us the fortitude to confront life's adversities but also compels us to share the incredible message of Jesus Christ with those yearning for redemption. Through our faith, we actively engage in God's divine plan of redemption, emerging as beacons of hope and inspiring others to embark on their journey to redemption and salvation through faith in Jesus Christ.

SEE THE STORY IN LUKE 2:36-38

23

THE FAITH OF THE BLEEDING WOMAN

As Jesus and His disciples made their way to the village of Capernaum, a tangible sense of excitement and anticipation filled the air. The news of the healer's imminent arrival had spread like wildfire, sparking a buzz among the people. People from all walks of life were pouring in from far and wide, drawn to the prospect of witnessing Jesus' transformative power firsthand, through His teachings and miracles. According to God's promise to Abraham, Jesus had come to bless all nations, and it was this promise that was now being fulfilled.

Those who believed in Him would be forgiven by God of their sins, healed from illnesses, and liberated from bondage. Jesus' ultimate purpose was to bring good news to the poor, set the captive free, give sight to the blind, and free the oppressed from the yoke of oppression (see Luke 4:18-19).

Jarius calls on Jesus in Desperation.

As Jesus stood before the crowd, His voice rose above the chatter and reached every ear. It was powerful, yet gentle, and carried an air of calm that soothed the hearts of those who listened. He spoke in parables, weaving together stories that contained hidden truths and profound wisdom. With each word, He explored the mysteries of the Kingdom of God, inviting those around Him to join Him on a journey of discovery.

His teachings captivated the people, and they hung on to every word that fell from His lips. They leaned in, eager to hear more, their hearts open and their minds receptive. But just as Jesus was reaching the climax of His message, a sudden cry shattered the moment's peace.

It was a desperate cry, full of pain and anguish, and it came from a man named Jarius. He pushed his way through the crowd, his eyes wild with desperation, and shouted out in a voice that shook the ground beneath their feet. "My daughter has died," he cried, "But come and put your hand on her, and she will live" (Matthew 9:18). The words echoed through the air, bouncing back and forth between the people until they seemed to fill the entire space. It was a moment of desperation and hope, of fear and faith, as Jarius clung to the belief that Jesus could perform a miracle and bring his daughter back to life.

The Faith of the Bleeding Woman

The man's faith and desperation moved Jesus, so He stood up to visit his daughter. Among the crowd was a woman who had been suffering from constant bleeding for 12 long years. She lay unnoticed in the shadows, silently hoping Jesus would notice and heal her. Her desperation must have been intense, as

THE FAITH OF THE BLEEDING WOMAN

she longed to be freed from suffering and made whole again. Amid the bustling crowd, where bodies pressed against each other in anticipation, this woman clung to a glimmer of hope. She yearned for Jesus to walk in her direction. However, her heart sank as she watched Jesus walk away, accompanying Jarius to his home.

The woman's physical and emotional weakness must have been evident. She had exhausted all options, seeking relief from numerous physicians, only to find her condition worsening. Nevertheless, determined not to return home unchanged, a spark of faith and determination ignited within her, giving her the courage to summon every ounce of strength she had. She mustered the will to drag herself towards Jesus. I imagine her with trembling limbs, extending her hand and pushing through the crowd until her fingertips brushed against the hem of Jesus' cloak. At that moment, it seemed as though a sudden burst of wind had swept away twelve years of sorrow, finally ending her suffering and pain. A transformation swept through her, leaving her with faith in Jesus as the true healer.

Immense joy and excitement must have filled her heart as she stood in awe of this miraculous change. Her body regained strength and vitality, breathing new life into her tired soul.

Jesus, sensing that power had left Him, asked who had touched Him. His disciples looked at Him in confusion, as many people were pushing against Him to catch a glimpse of Him. However, Jesus knew the woman had uniquely touched and drawn power from Him. However, the woman was hesitant to reveal her identity to Jesus. She had probably grown accustomed to hiding in the shadows and avoided drawing attention to herself due to her long illness. However, after experiencing Jesus' healing power, she stepped out of the shadows, and told Jesus the truth. I imagine that as she spoke, the nearby crowd listened attentively, and her testimony ignited their faith in Jesus.

Instead of rejecting her, Jesus affirmed her faith and spoke comfort and freedom, saying, "Daughter, your faith has healed you. Go in peace, and be freed from your suffering" (Mark 5:34).

The Role of the Faith of the Bleeding woman in God's Redemption Plan

The story of this woman who had been suffering from a chronic bleeding condition for years is nothing short of miraculous. Through her faith in Jesus Christ, she was healed, and not only did this bring about a physical transformation, but it also positioned her to play a significant role in God's narrative for redemption.

Her testimony of faith and healing is a compelling one, and it likely served as a source of inspiration for numerous individuals, prompting them to seek out Jesus and encounter His life-changing redemptive power for themselves. Even today, her faith in Jesus continues to inspire many.

Encouragement

> *"For it is by grace you have been saved, through faith—and this is not from yourselves, it is the gift of God."Ephesians 2:8*

The story of the bleeding woman, once hidden in

the shadows and weighed down by her affliction, is a powerful testimony of the transformative power of faith in Jesus. Her physical healing was a turning point that brought her out of the darkness and into the light, restoring her health and dignity and freeing her from the social stigma associated with her condition. However, her story is not just about physical healing. It is also a reminder that we all carry the weight of sin that plagues our lives and keeps us from experiencing true freedom. Unlike the woman who bled, we may not need physical healing, but we all need spiritual healing from the bondage of sin that enslaves us. Through faith in Jesus, we can be set free from the power of sin and death and experience true freedom and peace.

It's important to understand that Jesus may not always heal us from physical illnesses. He healed the bleeding woman out of compassion and grace, but He also allowed His disciples to suffer from various illnesses and even die for His sake. However, He will always free us from the bondage of sin and assure us of eternal life. This is because, through Jesus' death on the cross, He took on Himself the punishment and wrath of God that we deserved (see 2 Corinthians 5:21). He bore our sins on the cross and made it possible for us to be reconciled to God and have eternal life. This means that even though we may experience pain and suffering in this world, we will never have to suffer the pain of eternal separation from God. By putting our faith in Jesus, we too become a part of God's redemptive embrace.

SEE THE STORY IN MATTHEW 9: 20-22; MARK 5: 25-34; LUKE 8: 43-48

A THREAD OF FAITH

24

THE FAITH OF THE CANAANITE WOMAN

The Canaanites were an ancient civilization that thrived in the Canaan region, now modern-day Lebanon, Syria, Israel, and Palestine. They had a polytheistic society, which means they believed in and worshiped many gods and goddesses. On the other hand, the Israelites, who were descendants of Abraham, were a monotheistic society that only believed in the one true God, Yahweh — the Creator of the universe. This difference in religious beliefs created a fundamental conflict between the two societies.

The Canaanites and the Israelites often clashed over territory and resources. The Israelites believed God had promised Abraham that his descendants would inherit the land of Canaan, and they considered themselves the rightful owners of the land. This claim to the land was a significant point of contention between the two societies, leading to many conflicts and wars. Despite the hostility between the two societies, the Israelites eventually conquered the Canaanites and established their kingdom in the region. The biblical book of Joshua records this conquest, stating that God fulfilled His promise to Abraham by granting his descendants the land of Canaan (see Joshua 21:43).

Jesus Meets a Canaanite Woman

During His ministry, Jesus traveled to the districts of Tyre and Sidon, where He encountered a Canaanite woman, who was on the brink of experiencing His transformative power and blessing. At that time, Jesus had just concluded a teaching session with His disciples on the importance of what comes out of a person's mouth over what goes into their body. He emphasized that one's words reflect the actual state of one's heart (see Matthew 15:15-20).

As Jesus was walking, the Canaanite woman approached Him with desperation, crying out, "Lord, Son of David, have mercy on me! My daughter is demon-possessed and suffering terribly" (Matthew 15:22). Despite being associated with idolatry and wickedness due to her identity, the woman sought Jesus' mercy. She acknowledged Him as Lord and approached Him with faith that He alone could heal her daughter.

Amid religious and cultural tensions, the Israelites considered the Canaanite woman impure due to her idolatry. The Israelites questioned her worthiness because she did not worship the God of Creation, who had set apart the Israelites. Her words left Jesus' disciples astounded when they heard her, as they wondered how she could claim Jesus as her Lord, being an idolater. However, Jesus listened silently to His disciples as they urged Him to send her away, considering her unworthy of His attention. Jesus explained to the woman that God had sent Him to the descendants of Abraham, Israel's lost sheep.

The Faith of the Canaanite Woman

Jesus' words must have devastated the woman, as they suggested that He would deny her plea for help. Nevertheless, she refused to lose hope and begged even more fervently for Jesus to show mercy and heal her daughter. Jesus responded, and this time, he spoke to her sternly and uncompromisingly, telling her that it was not right to take the food meant for the children and throw it to the dogs. Jesus said this to emphasize further His point that He ministered only to the Israelites, who are the chosen people of God, and He did not minister to the unclean people who did not worship the God of Israel.

The woman, who was likely aware of the societal norms that dictated her status as an unclean Gentile, must have felt the sting of those words. Yet, she did not give up. Instead, she humbled herself even further and replied, "But even the dogs eat the crumbs that fall from their master's table" (Matthew 15:27). Jesus looked at her with compassion and recognized the strength of her faith, which transcended all boundaries and limitations. In that moment, He saw in her something more remarkable than her ethnicity or societal standing — a faith that radiated from the depths of her heart. With deep respect, Jesus declared, "Woman, you have great faith! Your request is granted" (Matthew 15:28). Just like that, the woman's faith became the saving grace for her daughter, bringing forth healing and restoration. Through her faith, the woman witnessed God's saving grace and became a part of His redemption.

The Role of the Canaanite Woman's Faith in God's Redemption

The story of the Canaanite woman powerfully reminds us of the lesson Jesus taught his disciples. In Matthew 15:11, Jesus addressed the crowd and declared, "Listen and understand. What goes into someone's mouth does not defile them, but what comes out of their mouth that is what defiles them."

He used this parable in response to the Pharisees' accusation against the disciples, who habitually did not wash their hands before eating bread (see Matthew 15:2).

The Pharisees believed that righteousness was external. They believed that performing certain rituals and outward actions were the ultimate defining factors of a person's righteousness. The Pharisees interpreted God's commands legalistically and missed the heart of the issue. However, Jesus emphasized that all sins come from the state of our hearts. Evil thoughts, murder, adultery, sexual immorality, theft, false testimony, and slander are what defile a person. He emphasized that righteousness' true essence is inward, not based on external actions or rituals.

Similarly, the Canaanite woman was deemed unclean by many because of her ethnicity. Despite the discrimination and prejudice she faced, she showed great faith and persistence. Her words revealed that her heart was in a different state than what her identity and ethnicity implied, and because of her faith-filled heart, she experienced God's redemption.

Encouragement

"So in Christ Jesus, you are all children of God through faith." Galatians 3:26

Like the Canaanite woman, many of us are outcasts and unclean because of our idolatry, wickedness, and various sins. We have not devoted ourselves to God or submitted our lives to His authority. Some of us, like the Canaanite woman, are not Israelites by birth, and our ancestors turned to foreign gods. As a result, we have been disobedient to the God of Israel for a long time, making us enemies of God. Therefore, we don't deserve to receive His mercy and grace. However, through our faith in Jesus Christ, the promised descendant of Abraham, we are welcomed into God's family and become part of His chosen people (see 1 Peter 2:9).

When Jesus granted the request of the Canaanite woman, it did not mean that He had changed His commitment to serving only God's chosen people. Instead, even though she was considered unclean because of her Canaanite heritage, her faith in Jesus cleansed her. It made her acceptable, allowing her to join God's family. Similarly, God can include anyone in His chosen people and make them descendants of Abraham. Faith is the only requirement, regardless of whether one is born Jewish or not.

In Galatians 3:26-29, the author emphasizes that the fundamental aspect of our redemption lies in our faith in Jesus Christ, which makes us spiritual heirs of Abraham. This spiritual inheritance means we can connect with the same promises and blessings that God granted to Abraham and his descendants. By having faith in Jesus Christ, we can overcome our outcast status, impurity, and all other barriers that keep us from being part of God's family.

SEE THE STORY IN MATTHEW 15:21-28

25

THE FAITH OF THE SAMARITAN WOMAN

The term "Samaritan" in the Bible refers to a person from the Samaria region, located north of Jerusalem. During the time of Jesus, the Jews who resided in Galilee and Judea were known to avoid interactions with Samaritans due to their religious differences. The Jews considered Samaritans to be people of mixed race who held impure and half-pagan beliefs. This conflict between Jews and Samaritans has its roots in ancient times. In 721 BC, the Assyrians conquered the northern kingdom of Israel, which led to the exile of many Israelites and the influx of people from other regions. The newcomers intermarried with the remaining Israelites, leading to the creation of a mixed-race population in Samaria. This mingling of cultures and religions led to the development of a unique Samaritan identity distinct from mainstream Judaism.

Jesus' Encounter with the Samaritan Woman

One day, as Jesus was traveling towards Galilee, He passed through the town of Sychar, located in Samaria. While on His way, He felt exhausted and decided to rest at Jacob's well. A Samaritan woman arrived at the well to draw water. When she saw Jesus, she was taken aback to find a Jew in Samaria, and she was even more surprised when Jesus requested her for some water to drink. Aware of the complex relationship between Jews and Samaritans, she questioned Jesus' request. However, He responded by telling her that if only she knew who was asking for water, she would have, instead, asked Him for living water, which He would joyfully provide.

As the woman carefully observed Jesus and tried to understand His words, her eyes were fixed on Him. She couldn't help but notice that He had nothing to draw water with, which puzzled her. How could He possibly give her the water He spoke of? Intrigued by His response, she couldn't contain her curiosity and asked Him how He would provide this water.

Jesus, perceiving the woman's deepest need, responded with a profound statement. He explained that the water He offers is unlike any other. It is a source of eternal satisfaction, quenching the soul's thirst. Whoever drinks this water will never thirst again, but instead, it will become a wellspring within them, leading to everlasting life. Although the woman didn't fully grasp the meaning behind Jesus' words, she was captivated by the idea of never experiencing thirst again. Eagerly, she requested this water, longing for a life free from the physical and spiritual thirst that plagued her.

Jesus Reveals Himself

At that moment, Jesus began to reveal the

significance of their encounter to her. He asked her personal questions, delving into the depths of her heart, and shared information that no one else could have known. The woman must have been astonished, realizing she was conversing with a prophet with divine insight. As their conversation continued, the woman expressed her faith in the coming Messiah, the Christ. She described that the Messiah is the one who would bring salvation and hope to the world. Jesus responded, catching the woman off guard. He declared, "I, the one speaking to you — I am he" (John 4:26).

I imagine these words echoed in her mind, causing her heart to race rapidly. Standing before her was not just a prophet but the long-awaited Messiah, fulfilling ancient prophecies. The figure that the prophets of old could only speak of was now standing in her presence.

The Faith of the Samaritan Woman

At that very moment, Jesus' disciples returned from their duties only to discover an unexpected sight.

Standing beside Jesus was an impure Samaritan woman with whom Jesus was not supposed to associate. The woman left her water jar behind without uttering a single word and rushed back to her community. She felt an overwhelming urgency to share what had just happened, causing her feet to move as quickly as they could carry her. Although her initial purpose was to fetch water, she returned bearing something far more precious — the revelation of the living water of life.

I can picture her cheerfully recounting the events to everyone she encountered, her words flowing like a rushing river. She exclaimed, "Come, see a man who told me everything I ever did. Could this be the Messiah?" (John 4:29).

The Role of the Faith of the Samaritan Woman in God's Plan of Redemption

As the Samaritan woman's powerful testimony reached the ears of her fellow Samaritans, it ignited a flame of faith in their hearts. Intrigued and moved, they eagerly accompanied her to meet Jesus in person. After personally hearing His teachings and witnessing His presence, they expressed to her, "We no longer believe just because of what you said; now we have heard for ourselves, and we know that this man is the Savior of the world" (John 4:42).

The faith of the Samaritan woman played a crucial role in God's divine plan, not only in her redemption but also in bringing redemption to her entire community through faith in Jesus Christ.

Encouragement

> *"Whoever believes in me, as Scripture has said, rivers of living water will flow from within them." John 7:38*

The woman's story from Samaria is a powerful example of the transformative power of faith in Jesus Christ. Before joining God's family, she faced marginalization from her community and was considered an outcast by the Jewish people. However, her encounter with Jesus changed everything. Through her faith in Him, she found salvation and was accepted and valued by Jesus Christ, even though she was from a different culture and background.

The woman's dedication and commitment to spreading the message of the Messiah resulted in many people embracing faith in Jesus. God used her faith as an essential part of His plan for redemption, and she became an instrumental figure in sharing the good news of salvation with others.

Her story reminds us that, no matter our flaws, struggles, or societal rejection, Jesus reaches out to us with love, and invites us to have a relationship with God through faith in Him. As believers, we have an essential role in God's grand plan for redemption. We must share this incredible news with everyone we meet, just as the woman from Samaria did, and invite them to experience the life-changing power of faith in Jesus Christ. By doing so, we can help others find salvation and become part of God's family.

SEE THE STORY IN JOHN 4:5-30

26

THE FAITH OF MARY OF BETHANY

Mary of Bethany, a woman well-known for her faith and deep devotion, had the incredible privilege of being a close companion of Jesus Himself. As the sister of Martha and Lazarus, Mary had the unique opportunity to spend quality time with Jesus, personally listening to His teachings. Whenever Jesus spoke, Mary would eagerly sit at His feet, entirely captivated by His every word (see Luke 10:39).

One day, Jesus came to their home, and Mary's

heart was filled with an overwhelming passion for Jesus. Even though she had heard Jesus teach countless times, this moment felt different. It was as if Mary began to understand that Jesus was not just an ordinary teacher but the long-awaited Messiah promised by the prophets of old. Mary's faith soared in that moment, and her love and devotion for her Savior overflowed.

When Jesus arrived, Mary had an extraordinary plan in mind. She was determined to express her utmost honor and devotion to Jesus, regardless of any criticism she might face. She planned to use an alabaster box filled with precious ointments and oils to honor Jesus. In Jewish tradition, an alabaster box was typically given to young girls as a symbol of their maturity for marriage, with its size representing the dowry for the daughter.

The box held immense value and significance, as it contained oils worth an entire year's wages. However, the value of the precious oils and the container paled in comparison to the immense price Jesus would soon pay to win Mary's heart and make her His radiant bride.

The Faith of Mary of Bethany

As Mary broke her alabaster box at Jesus' feet, the air was filled with the captivating fragrance of luxurious perfumes, overpowering every other scent. Unfazed by the disapproving stares and hushed whispers that labeled her a sinner, she remained steadfast in her act of devotion to Jesus. The Pharisees, who could not comprehend how someone with such a tainted reputation could dare to touch Jesus' feet, looked on with disgust. However, Mary's heart overflowed with emotions, as if she could already see Jesus, stripped and crucified, bearing the weight of her sins. Tears streamed down her face as she humbly used her hair to wipe Jesus' feet. Deep within her, Mary held onto faith that Jesus would not turn her away, regardless of her sins or what others thought of her. As she anointed Jesus' feet with her precious perfume, her love and surrender to Jesus shone through, illuminating the room.

A significant ceremony involves breaking an alabaster box. This ceremony occurs when a man proposes marriage to a woman and seeks her family's approval. During the ceremony, the woman shatters the box and anoints the man's feet with perfume, symbolizing her honor and acceptance of his request.

In the same way, Jesus' crucifixion symbolized a deep marriage proposal, not only for Mary but for all humanity. The proposal calls for everyone to unite with Him through faith and have an eternal relationship with Him and God. Remarkably, even before Jesus formally extended the proposal on the cross, Mary embraced and accepted it. In response to her surrender, Jesus declared, "Your faith has saved you; go in peace" (see Luke 7:50).

The Role of Mary of Bethany's Faith in God's Redemption Plan

After Mary performed this act of devotion, Jesus acknowledged that her actions would be remembered and spoken of for generations to come, wherever the Gospel was shared (see Matthew 26:13). Her act of faith and devotion outlived her, leaving a lasting impact that highlights the powerful ripple effects of faith. As Jesus faced the overwhelming pain and suffering of His approaching crucifixion, one cannot help but wonder if He could still smell the lingering fragrance of the luxurious perfumes Mary had used to anoint Him. This scent may have served as a powerful reminder of the purpose for which He was sacrificing His life — to bring about a new covenant and to redeem a Bride in each of us who would have faith in Him and submit to His authority and love. Mary's devotion was a powerful symbol of the kind of faith that Jesus calls us to have — one that is willing to surrender everything at His feet.

Encouragement

> *"If you declare with your mouth, "Jesus is Lord," and believe in your heart that God raised him from the dead, you will be saved. For it is with your heart that you believe and are justified, and it is with your mouth that you profess your faith and are saved." Romans*

THE FAITH OF MARY OF BETHANY

10:9-10

The Gospel message is centered on the remarkable truth that Jesus willingly took upon Himself the punishment for our sins, as an act of love and sacrifice. By placing our faith in Him, we are saved from eternal damnation and granted everlasting life. This incredible gift of salvation allows us to experience an intimate and personal relationship with God and frees us from the condemnation that comes with sin.

By putting our trust in Jesus and surrendering our lives to Him, we can rest assured that He will never reject us, just as He did not reject Mary. Instead, He accepts us with His open arms, cleansing us from our sins so that, we can become His radiant bride without any spot or blemish (see Ephesians 5:25-28). The transformation that comes from accepting His gift of salvation is truly remarkable, as we experience the power of His grace and find true fulfillment in Him.

If you have yet to consider putting your faith in

Jesus Christ, know that He offers forgiveness for all sins and can transform your life with His love. By accepting His gift of salvation and embracing the Gospel message, you can experience the fullness of life that He offers, and enjoy the peace, joy, and love that comes with being united with Him (see Romans 3:21-31).

SEE THE STORY IN MATTHEW 26:6-11

27

THE FAITH OF MARY MAGDALENE

The promise made by God to Abraham found its fulfillment in Jesus Christ (see Acts 4:10-12; Galatians 3:16). However, despite being the promised Messiah (see Matthew 1:16), Jesus was rejected by His people, the Israelites, who failed to recognize Him as the long-awaited Messiah sent by God (see John 10:20; John 7:12-13). The Hebrew term "Messiah," derived from "mashiaḥ," means "anointed." The Messiah was expected to be a king from the lineage of David, who would free Israel from foreign oppression and restore the nation to its former glory.

John the Baptist identified Jesus as the Messiah and sent his messengers to inquire whether Jesus was indeed the Christ (Messiah). Jesus clarified that He was the Messiah, but His purpose was different from what most people anticipated (see Luke 7:18-22; John 18:36).

Instead of leading a political uprising against Roman rule, under which the Israelites were, Jesus came to offer Himself as a sacrifice for the forgiveness of sins (see Luke 19:10; Hebrews 9:28).

The rejection of Jesus as the Messiah ultimately led to a conspiracy to have Him killed, and He was crucified, fulfilling the prophecy in Isaiah 53.

The crucifixion of Jesus

During the crucifixion of Jesus Christ, Mary Magdalene, along with a group of women, stood at a distance and witnessed the mocking, beating, and crucifixion of Jesus, who was being punished for the sins of the world. Mary had the privilege of being a close follower of Jesus, walking alongside Him as one of His disciples. She listened intently to His teachings and witnessed His miraculous healings and deliverances, which left her in awe of His power and wisdom. As a devoted follower of Jesus, Mary had become dependent on His leadership and guidance in all aspects of life. She had given up everything to follow Him and had developed a deep trust and faith in Him and His teachings. However, on this day, it must have been unimaginable for her to witness the brutal treatment and eventual death of the man she had come to love and respect.

As Mary stood there, overwhelmed with grief, she watched as Jesus took His last breath. She knew that there was nothing she could do to rescue Him; all she could do was stand there and bear witness to the tragic events unfolding before her eyes. It was a moment of profound sadness and despair as Mary and the other followers of Jesus struggled to come to terms with the loss of their beloved leader.

Joseph Requested Jesus' Body

As the night grew darker, a heavy silence enveloped the land, mirroring the weight of grief in the air. The scattered and disheartened disciples retreated to their hiding places; their hearts were heavy with sorrow and confusion. Yet amidst the despair, Joseph of Arimathea, a secret follower of Jesus, found the courage to approach Pontius Pilate, the Roman governor who had condemned their beloved teacher to death. Joseph stood before Pilate, and he pleaded to give Jesus a proper burial.

Pilate, perhaps moved by Joseph's sincerity, granted Joseph permission to take Jesus' lifeless body. With utmost care and tenderness, Joseph approached the cross where Jesus had been crucified. He gently removed the nails that held Jesus' hands and feet, cradling the lifeless form in his arms. Joseph further wrapped Jesus' body in fresh linen, meticulously ensuring that every inch was covered. He respectfully placed the body in his newly carved tomb made from solid rock. To secure the resting place, Joseph rolled a large stone before the tomb's entrance and left.

Meanwhile, Mary Magdalene and other women sat nearby, their hearts burdened with grief. The air was filled with the sounds of mourning and crying as they looked at the stone that now enclosed their beloved teacher's lifeless body. Jesus' death did not turn away Mary; she remained loyal to Him even in death, showing her deep devotion to Jesus Christ. Despite their sorrow, I imagine Mary and the other women found comfort in knowing where Jesus' body was.

On the next day, the Pharisees, who had questioned Jesus' declaration that He would be crucified and then rise again after three days, approached Pilate. They asked him to place guards at the tomb, fearing that one of Jesus' followers might steal the body and falsely claim that Jesus had indeed come back to life. Pilate agreed to their request.

The Faith of Mary Magdalene

On the day following the Sabbath, the first day of the week, Mary and other women decided to visit Jesus' tomb. They carried with them some aromatic spices to anoint the body of Jesus. As they made their way toward the tomb, their hearts were heavy with grief and consumed with thoughts of how they would manage to move the massive stone that sealed it. Upon their arrival, they were surprised to find that the stone had already been moved, granting them access to the tomb. As they drew closer, they were greeted by an angel informing them that Jesus had risen from the dead.

As the angel instructed them, the women stood before him in utter amazement. The news they had just received was too incredible to comprehend. I imagine their eyes widened, their hearts raced, and their knees trembled. The angel's words had wiped away the tears they had shed in the previous days and mended their broken hearts. As the women exchanged astonished glances, their minds raced to remember Jesus' teachings about His crucifixion and resurrection. It was as if a light bulb suddenly illuminated their understanding of the angel's message.

The women quickly left the tomb, filled with hope and faith in the angel's message. They hurriedly carried this incredible news with them as they made their way to the disciples. The Pharisees' attempts to stop the resurrection had failed, and the truth of Jesus' victory over sin and death shone brightly for all to see.

The Role of Mary's Faith in God's Redemption Plan

Mary's encounter with Jesus was a life-changing experience that ignited a deep faith and dedication within her. Mary's journey did not end there. Her faith in Jesus continued to grow, and she became an integral part of God's plan for redemption.

Mary Magdalene was at a crossroads when she received the angel's message about Jesus' resurrection — the moment demanded a choice between unbelief and faith. Despite the overwhelming nature of the situation, Mary's belief in Jesus propelled her to choose faith.

In that moment, Mary could have easily succumbed to doubt and skepticism. The idea of Jesus rising from the dead seemed impossible. Doubt could have clouded her mind, causing her to question the authenticity of the angel's message. But Mary, with her heart filled with faith and devotion, made a conscious decision to trust in the message from the angel.

This decision to have faith in the face of uncertainty transformed Mary's life forever. It was faith that led her to become one of the first women to bear witness to Jesus' resurrection. She did not shrink back in fear of being ridiculed and not believed by the disciples. Her faith and obedience to share the testimony of Jesus Christ allowed her to play an essential role in God's redemption plan, forever etching her name in history as a woman of faith and courage.

Encouragement

> *"Go into all the world and preach the gospel to all creation. Whoever believes and is baptized will be saved, but whoever does not believe will be condemned. And these signs will accompany those who believe: In my name, they will drive*

out demons; they will speak in new tongues; they will pick up snakes with their hands; and when they drink deadly poison, it will not hurt them at all; they will place their hands on sick people, and they will get well."
Mark 16:15-18

The message about Jesus Christ's resurrection, which the angel gave to Mary Magdalene, is the most significant message in Christianity. Just as the angel instructed Mary to share the good news that Jesus had overcome death and risen from the grave, we, as disciples of Jesus Christ, are also commanded to go out in faith and proclaim the Gospel message to the world.

As Christians, we believe that Jesus Christ's death and resurrection fulfill God's plan for redemption. This event represents the triumph of good over evil and life over death. It symbolizes hope and a promise of eternal life for all who believe in Jesus Christ. By sharing this message with others, we are fulfilling our role as disciples of Jesus and participating in God's plan for the redemption of all humanity.

Furthermore, the message of the death and resurrection of Jesus is not just a historical event that happened long ago. It is a message that is still relevant today and still transforming lives worldwide. As we proclaim this message, we become part of God's redemption plan that is still unfolding.

SEE THE STORY IN MARK 15:40-47; MARK 16:1-20

EPILOGUE

The women mentioned in this book serve as a reminder that God's plan of redemption goes beyond the extraordinary. He intentionally selects the weak, the outcasts, and the impure to demonstrate His incredible power to redeem. Their stories display the power of faith and the love and faithfulness of God in rescuing sinful individuals who are undeserving of His mercy and grace. Despite Eve's sinful condition and wavering faith, she witnessed God's steadfast faithfulness. God, who possesses complete knowledge, was fully aware of humanity's inclination towards sin, yet still chose to create us and devised a plan to redeem us from this sinful nature.

God's plan of redemption was revealed through Abraham's descendant, Jesus the Messiah. His selfless sacrifice on the cross allowed humanity to find salvation and establish a personal relationship with God through faith in Him. By embracing faith, we can experience the transformative love of God and become an inseparable part of the fabric of faith that God has interwoven throughout the lives of women who came before us. Unbeknownst to these women, their collective faith was instrumental in bringing forth God's plan of redemption, not only in their own lives but also in the lives of those around them and future generations. God invites us to join this unbroken thread of faith by wholeheartedly believing in Jesus Christ.

Therefore, are you ready to embark on a transformative journey of surrender and actively participate in God's captivating story of redemption through faith as His plan unfolds?

Believing in Jesus Christ as our Lord and Savior redeems us to the right standing with God. Despite once being separated from Him by sin, we can walk with God once again, just as Eve did in the Garden of Eden. By accepting Jesus, we can fully know God as our Heavenly Father and trust His goodness.

As we walk hand in hand with God, we experience freedom and contentment that cannot be found anywhere else. Our hearts overflow with joy and peace as we draw closer to God, knowing that He has forgiven us of all our sins and that, we have eternal life in Him. Our redemption becomes a way for God to redeem others, and our faith acts as a thread that God uses to weave His grand tapestry of reconciling all of humanity to Himself.

So, will you accept God's invitation to surrender your life to Him and become part of His plan of redemption? It's a journey worth taking that will transform your life forever.

PRAYER

Father, I am grateful for Your incredible plan of redemption and how You brought it to fruition through Jesus Christ. I am thankful that, by placing my faith in Him, my sins are forgiven, and I have the assurance of eternal life. Despite my impurity and undeserving of Your mercy, You have brought me into a deep relationship with You, where I can know You as my loving Father and the ruler of my life.

At this moment, I lift the woman reading this prayer to You, Father. I ask that You ignite faith within her heart. Let her understand that it was never Your intention for her to live a life filled with sin, pain, and suffering. Help her realize that, even amid her afflictions, You have a divine plan to redeem, restore, and deliver her through faith in Jesus Christ.

Open her eyes, Father, so that she may see this plan. Open her ears, so that she may hear Your voice and truly comprehend Your plan. Soften her heart, so that she may be receptive to the promptings of Your Holy Spirit, working within her to believe and trust in You. Only You, God, truly know that it was through faith that I wrote this book, and it is by that same faith that this book has found its way into her hands.

I pray, Father, that You bring Your precious daughter into a deep trust in Jesus Christ. Use her faith as a beautiful thread that You will weave into Your Story, a story of redemption, love, and grace. May her life be a testament to Your power and may she inspire others to place their faith in You as well. In Jesus' name, I pray, Amen.

ABOUT THE AUTHOR

Suprise Žihlavski, originally from South Africa, now resides in Serbia with her husband. She holds a degree in journalism and a certificate in theology. In her career as a Journalist, she has written about negative events plaguing society as well as those that inspire hope. However, Suprise has discovered a passion that surpasses all others. It is the joy she experiences when she tells stories that lead people to the good news of Jesus Christ.

Her most prized possessions are her faith and her family. Apart from spending time with her loved ones, she enjoys DIY projects, especially refurbishing old furniture.

A Thread of Faith is Suprise's debut book

ACKNOWLEDGMENTS

I want to express my gratitude to Jesus for empowering me to write this book. Special thanks to my husband, Vladimir, for his faith in me and constant encouragement. And a heartfelt thank you to all the amazing individuals who offered advice and prayers to help bring this book to life.

SCRIPTURES TO STRENGTHEN YOUR FAITH

- *Oh, taste and see that the Lord is good; Blessed is the man who trusts in Him! Oh, fear the Lord, you His saints! There is no want to those who fear Him. Psalm 34:8-9 (NKJV)*

- *For we live by faith, not by sight. 2 Corinthians 5:7*

- *As the body without the spirit is dead, so faith without deeds is dead. James 2:26*

- *But we do not belong to those who shrink back and are destroyed, but to those who have faith and are saved. Hebrews 10:39*

❖ *But I trust in your unfailing love; my heart rejoices in your salvation. Psalm 13:5*

❖ *The Lord is my rock, my fortress and my deliverer; my God is my rock, in whom I take refuge, my shield and the horn of my salvation, my stronghold. Psalm 18:2*

❖ *Those who know your name trust in you, for you, Lord, have never forsaken those who seek you. Psalm 9:10*

❖ *And without faith it is impossible to please God, because anyone who comes to him must believe that he exists and that he rewards those who earnestly seek him. Hebrews 11:6*

❖ *Be on your guard; stand firm in the faith; be courageous; be strong. 1 Corinthians*

16:13

❖ *The Lord is my strength and my shield; my heart trusts in him, and he helps me. Psalm 28:7*

❖ *Many are the woes of the wicked, but the Lord's unfailing love surrounds the one who trusts in him. Psalm 32:10*

❖ *We wait in hope for the Lord; he is our help and our shield. In him, our hearts rejoice, for we trust in his holy name. Psalm 33:20-21*

❖ *Trust in him at all times, you people; pour out your hearts to him, for God is our refuge. Psalm 62:8*

❖ *Trust in the Lord with all your heart and lean not on your own understanding. Proverbs 3:5*

www.ingramcontent.com/pod-product-compliance
Lightning Source LLC
Chambersburg PA
CBHW031441040426
42444CB00007B/917